At Issue

Should Character Be Taught in School?

Other Books in the At Issue Series:

At Issue

Should Character Be Taught in School?

Noël Merino, Book Editor

GREENHAVEN PRESS
A part of Gale, Cengage Learning

GALE
CENGAGE Learning

Detroit • New York • San Francisco • New Haven, Conn • Waterville, Maine • London

Christine Nasso, *Publisher*
Elizabeth Des Chenes, *Managing Editor*

© 2010 Greenhaven Press, a part of Gale, Cengage Learning.

Gale and Greenhaven Press are registered trademarks used herein under license.

For more information, contact:
Greenhaven Press
27500 Drake Rd.
Farmington Hills, MI 48331-3535
Or you can visit our Internet site at gale.cengage.com

For product information and technology assistance, contact us at

Gale Customer Support, 1-800-877-4253
For permission to use material from this text or product, submit all requests online at www.cengage.com/permissions

Further permissions questions can be emailed to permissionrequest@cengage.com

Articles in Greenhaven Press anthologies are often edited for length to meet page requirements. In addition, original titles of these works are changed to clearly present the main thesis and to explicitly indicate the author's opinion. Every effort is made to ensure that Greenhaven Press accurately reflects the original intent of the authors. Every effort has been made to trace the owners of copyrighted material.

Cover image © Todd Davidson/Illustration Works/Corbis.

LIBRARY OF CONGRESS CATALOGING-IN-PUBLICATION DATA

Should character be taught in school? / Noël Merino, book editor.
    p. cm. -- (At issue)
    Includes bibliographical references and index.
    ISBN 978-0-7377-4890-1 (hardcover) -- ISBN 978-0-7377-4891-8 (pbk.)
    1. Moral education--Juvenile literature. 2. Character--Study and teaching--United States. I. Merino, Noël.
    LC268.S464 2010
    370.11'4--dc22
                                    2010007134

Printed in the United States of America
1 2 3 4 5 6 7 14 13 12 11 10

Contents

Introduction

The debate about character education centers on one main question: Is school the appropriate place for young people to learn about the development of moral character? Although in the past the general consensus was that the answer to this question was yes, widespread disagreement now exists. Even those who answer affirmatively have a variety of competing proposals for what character education should entail. One of the main issues here, especially for public schools, is the extent to which religion should play a role, if any. The history of character education in the United States shows how views about character education evolved over time, resulting in the present-day debate.

The idea that the development of character is an important component of learning goes back many centuries. The ancient Greek philosophers, most notably Aristotle, talked extensively about the importance of character, noting that building an excellent character requires practice: "Excellence is an art won by training and habituation. We do not act rightly because we have virtue or excellence, but we rather have those because we have acted rightly. We are what we repeatedly do. Excellence, then, is not an act but a habit." Since the time of the ancient Greeks, the young have always been the focus of this education: at home and in religious services. During the time when parents were the main providers of education, the inclusion of moral education alongside other education was not controversial—rather it was expected. With the rise of public schools, however, character education made its way outside the home and church.

During the eighteenth-century colonial period in the United States, schooling was quite a bit different than it is today. Most people lived in small communities and the population was fairly homogeneous. School was not free, and the attendees were primarily boys and young men. According to scholar Ronald E. Galbraith, during that period school textbooks centered exclusively on moral and religious content. The most popular educational textbook of those days was *The New England Primer*, which taught reading and grammar through religious maxims and moral lessons. One passage of the 1777 text reads,

"Good children must,

Fear God all day, Love Christ alway,

Parents obey, In secret pray,

No false thing say, Mind little play,

By no sin stray, Make no delay,

In doing good."

Among the heavily Protestant immigrants of the day, such a focus on religious character education was desirable and relatively uncontroversial.

Public schools flourished in the nineteenth century in the United States and by 1870, taxes supported schools. During this period, new immigrants challenged the widespread Protestant schooling, though without challenging the need for character education itself. Meanwhile, the Bible became less popular in classrooms, since the various religious groups could not agree on a version. Nonetheless, the religious influence and focus on moral education continued with widespread use of the McGuffey Readers, which—like *The New England Primer*—focused on reading through moral tales. Millions of copies were sold in the nineteenth century, and they became the standard textbooks in most states after the Civil War.

By the early twentieth century, most states had compulsory attendance laws and the majority of American children attended school. As the American population became more diverse, the separation between church and state was pursued more strongly within the public schools. During this time, many states passed Blaine Amendments, which forbid the use of government money in educational institutions with religious affiliation. In reality, these amendments were not an attempt to secularize education but mainly an attempt to keep federal funds from going to Catholic schools, which were seen as a threat to the dominant Protestantism. After the U.S. Supreme Court ruled in 1925 that children could attend private schools and still comply with compulsory education laws, religious schooling drifted away from public schools toward private ones. In the latter half of the twentieth century, more and more of the American public started to view any teaching of morality, religious or otherwise, as an improper goal for the public schools.

In the last few decades, the call for character education has seen a resurgence, from both religious and secular groups. Some claim that the decline in character education over the years has led to an increase in crime and other social problems. Others see character education as intimately connected with the goals of education in general. Alongside this renewed interest in character education, however, is widespread concern that such character education is a thinly veiled attempt to bring religion into the public schools, in violation of the constitutional mandate for the separation of church and state. These are some of the issues that the viewpoints in *At Issue: Should Character Be Taught in School?* cover.

1

Character Education Is Needed in Public Schools

Charles C. Haynes and Marvin W. Berkowitz

Charles C. Haynes is a senior scholar at the First Amendment Center in Washington, D.C. Marvin W. Berkowitz is the Sanford N. McDonnell Professor of Character Education at the University of Missouri, St. Louis.

Americans have focused too much on students' test scores and too little on building character in schools. Character education does not need to compete with academics—actually, it can enhance it. A Missouri middle school that adopted character education and turned a failing school into a successful one provides an example of how character education can lead to success. More public schools should be implementing comprehensive plans for character education to improve both the morals and the academic performance of students.

After the endless headlines involving corrupt politicians, corporate cheats, doped-up sports stars and Internet predators, you might think that the American people would be demanding more character education in schools.

Think again.

"Good character," like the weather, gets a lot of talk—but too little action. We bemoan the loss of integrity and lack of responsibility in American public life. We decry the numbing statistics about teenage substance abuse, sexual promiscuity and gang activity. We wring our hands over surveys that report widespread cheating in schools and colleges. And then we move on to more important things.

Test scores, for example.

That's right: Standardized test results seem to trump everything else in education these days. No matter how many warning bells are sounded about the crisis of character in our society and despite the long-standing understanding that education is for the whole child, all we want to hear is how each school did on the exam.

Reading and math are important, but if we care about our kids (and our future) shouldn't we be paying more attention to the kinds of human beings who do the math and read the books?

"To educate a person in mind and not in morals," said Theodore Roosevelt, "is to educate a menace to society."

Fortunately, taking academics and character seriously in schools isn't an either/or proposition. Done well, character development enhances academic performance. Just ask Kristen Pelster, principal of Ridgewood Middle School, a rural/suburban school of about 503 students (42% of them economically disadvantaged) in Arnold, Missouri.

When Pelster arrived as assistant principal six years ago, Ridgewood had all the marks of the proverbial "failing school": high absenteeism, low academic achievement and a constant stream of discipline problems. Located in a poor community plagued by inadequate housing and meth labs, the school had graffiti on the walls, profanity echoing in the halls and a rusty chain fence surrounding it. It could have been the movie set for *Blackboard Jungle*.

Working as a team, Pelster and then principal Tim Crutchley, who was also new, made a commitment to transform Ridgewood. First, they diagnosed the problem: Students didn't feel as though anyone cared about them or the school.

Then they articulated a vision for "a school where there is caring, a sense of belonging and academic achievement."

Facing angry parents and a dispirited staff, Crutchley and Pelster knew they had much convincing to do. When they first arrived at Ridgewood, dozens of parents had requested that their children be moved to another school. Step One was to clean up the physical environment (the rusty fence was the first thing to go).

Fortunately, taking academics and character seriously in schools isn't an either/or proposition.

Initially, "caring" was a lot like "tough love." Crutchley and Pelster raised the bar on attendance, often going to truant students' homes to bring them to school. They established a "failure is not an option" program that prohibited the giving of zeros for missing work. Students had to make up missing homework during lunch hour. Teachers were required to integrate character education into academic lessons and behavior management.

By the end of the first year, the two leaders had won over a core team of teachers, critical support that, with the help of parents and members of the community, let the school progress.

How It Works

The Ridgewood activists learned early on that "character education" is far more than slogans or quick-fix lessons about a word of the week. To be effective, character education must become integral to the daily actions of everyone in the school community.

It starts with the faculty. Early in the process, Crutchley and Pelster drove out teachers who didn't show concern for students and recruited teachers who did.

They allocated resources to provide staff development. This modest investment in teacher training—a few thousand dollars—constituted almost the entire cost to implement their plan.

To be effective, character education must become integral to the daily actions of everyone in the school community.

Effective character education is not an add-on, but instead uses "teachable moments" in every classroom. Seventh-grade teacher Kacie Heiken, for example, has her students write and illustrate fairy tales that have a positive moral lesson. The students go to elementary schools and read their stories to classes before donating the books to a local children's hospital.

In American history classes, students study veterans, war and military service, culminating in a schoolwide celebration of Veterans Day that includes breakfast and a patriotic slide show for local veterans and their families.

Science students recently collaborated with a local church group to build a nature trail.

Ridgewood's effort extends beyond the curriculum. For half an hour each day, students meet with an adult mentor in small, family-like advisory groups. "The advisory helps form strong relationships between staff and student and among students. It creates a sense of being more of a family than an institution," Crutchley says.

But character education at Ridgewood isn't solely, or even predominantly, a top-down process. Daily class meetings include ethics discussions led by students. A one-semester course in "teen leadership" prepares students to take the lead in implementing an honor code and dealing with problems such as bullying.

Parents also play a key role. After all, they have primary responsibility for the moral development of their kids. While some parents have abdicated this responsibility, most want schools to reinforce and model the moral values taught at home. Many Ridgewood parents now volunteer at the school, and attendance at parent conferences has risen from 44.5% in 2000 to 75% in 2005.

A "New" School

Today, Crutchley is assistant superintendent of the district and Pelster, now principal, presides over a transformed Ridgewood.

Academic performance is up, disciplinary referrals are down by more than 70%, and the student failure rate has dropped to zero. Attendance has also improved, with the formerly daily home visits for truant students now down to four or five per year.

The rusty fence and graffiti are long gone, replaced by displays of student class work and high expectations: Ridgewood has been on Missouri's list of Top Ten Most Improved Schools for four of the past five years.

In October, Ridgewood was one of 10 schools and districts in the nation to be recognized as a 2006 National School of Character by the Character Education Partnership.

Character education is making a comeback.

Ridgewood's turnaround may be unusual, but it is not unique. "Schools of Character," schools that are implementing a comprehensive plan for character education, can be found in school districts across the USA. No study has yet been done on how many schools are providing character education, but the need is clear and the interest is understandably immense.

Ridgewood is a remarkable case study, but the success of character education is well documented. It works.

Victor Battistich of the University of Missouri–St. Louis, examined all the scientific research of the past 15 years and concluded that "comprehensive, high-quality character education" can prevent a wide range of problems, including "aggressive and antisocial behaviors, drug use, precocious sexual activity, criminal activities, academic underachievement and school failure."

Change Is Coming

So why aren't all schools doing it? In the early history of public education, developing good character was seen as an essential part of preparing people for citizenship in a democratic society. But in the latter part of the 20th century, many public schools moved away from the traditional emphasis on character and citizenship as American society grew more complex and diverse.

Today, character education is making a comeback. Thirty-one states mandate or encourage character education by statute. While pronouncements by legislatures don't necessarily translate into quality character education programs, it's a start.

Much is at stake in getting this right. At this critical moment in America's history, we need far more than higher math and reading scores. We need citizens who have the strength of character to uphold democratic freedom in the face of unprecedented challenges at home and abroad.

"Only a virtuous people are capable of freedom," is the familiar aphorism from Benjamin Franklin. Less well-known, but worth recalling, is the warning in the sentence that follows: "As nations become corrupt and vicious, they have more need of masters."

2

Character Education Cannot Work in Public School

Doug McManaman

Doug McManaman is a deacon and an instructor of theology and philosophy at Father Michael McGivney Catholic Academy in Markham, Ontario, Canada.

Character education cannot be taught in public schools because of the lack of a social understanding of a single ultimate end. Given the fact that both Canadian and American societies embrace liberalism, allowing each person to determine the meaning of his or her existence, teachers in public schools have no way to teach virtue. Teaching virtue would necessitate embracing a shared vision, but without common ground, this shared vision does not exist. As such, teaching character will result in teaching a variety of different values, depending on the instructor, and so it does not work within a public, nonreligious school.

On my way home from work the other day, I drove past a public school with a billboard bearing the legend: Character Matters. Below it was written "courage," exhibited as the character trait of the month.

The Meaning of Virtue

I had to wonder exactly what a public school teacher would say constitutes courage, and how he would distinguish it from its fraudulent counterparts, for the school is not far from a

Doug McManaman, "Character Education in a Public School," *Catholic Insight*, vol. 14, no. 6, June 2006, pp. 20–21. Copyright © 2006 *Catholic Insight*. Reproduced by permission.

new development of expensive houses, and it is likely that some students could find the "courage" to skip school and rob one of them during the day. In light of the fact that teaching something definitive on the overall meaning of human life is a monumental *faux pas* [mistake] within the public school system, the problem is genuine; for one cannot so much as put up a small Christmas tree in a classroom without someone coming down hard and forbidding it.

But without an understanding of the overall meaning of human life, without a single ultimate end towards which human persons ought to direct their choices, virtues—such as courage, justice, self-control, patience, affability, self-sacrifice, chastity, and fidelity—will mean not only different things to different people, but more often than not, contradictory things.

Consider how many people in Canada deem Robert Latimer [who was convicted of second-degree murder in the death of his ill daughter] a courageous man for putting his daughter out of her misery and facing the judicial system for doing so. One university has honoured abortionist Henry Morgentaler as a man of exemplary virtue, a man of justice and courage who was willing to suffer through lawsuits and jail time so that "women could have justice." Fairness to the devoted socialist often amounts to serious human rights violations for the capitalist, and vice versa. Chastity for one male student might mean having sex with one girl only—his girlfriend—while to someone else, it might mean not having sex at all until marriage.

What exactly is the criterion by which a teacher can help students determine what in fact constitutes a truly brave, just, temperate, in short, virtuous character? For the Catholic teacher, there is no dilemma. There is one ultimate end for which human persons have been created: "Oh, Lord, you made us for yourselves, and our hearts are restless until they rest in Thee" (St. Augustine). In this light, it isn't entirely foolhardy to give your life for another. Why? Because death no longer has the final word over our lives, for Christ is risen. And a Catholic teacher can stand up and proclaim that "the man without love has known nothing of God, for God is love. . . . Love, then, consists in this: not that we have loved God, but that He has loved us and has sent his Son as an offering for our sins. Beloved, if God has loved us so, we must have the same love for one another" (1 Jn. [1 John (Epistle)] 4:8–11). In short, those choices inconsistent with love of the Supreme Good and thus an integral love of human goods are not virtuous.

Without a single ultimate end towards which human persons ought to direct their choices, virtues . . . will mean not only different things to different people, but more often than not, contradictory things.

Character Education and Liberalism

But public schools don't have the luxury of quoting the scriptures or speaking about God. And the problem is even more pronounced in light of *Planned Parenthood [of Southeastern Pennsylvania] v. Casey* [1992]. U.S. Supreme Court Justices [Sandra Day] O'Connor, [Anthony] Kennedy, and [David] Souter wrote: "At the heart of liberty is the right to define one's own concept of existence, of meaning, of the universe, and of the mystery of human life. Beliefs about these matters could not define the attributes of personhood were they formed under compulsion of the State."

Such sentiments have been at the heart of Canadian liberalism for decades now. Hence, there can be no shared vision on what constitutes a virtuous existence. As a free citizen, I have the right to decide that I am the ultimate meaning of my own existence, and that everyone else is a means to be used for that end. And since virtues are means whose meaning is determined by an end, prudence, justice, fortitude and temperance and all their parts will mean completely and utterly different things to different people.

In this light, character education in a postmodern culture is akin to urging a person to drive, but without saying where, or providing shoes for a person with no legs, or sailing without a compass. We are spinning our wheels, but with a semblance of moral respectability convincing ourselves that we are actually making people better without permitting anyone to establish for students just what the criteria for "good," "better" and "best" really are, leaving the question of the ultimate end entirely to the whims of each student.

Character education in a postmodern culture is akin to urging a person to drive, but without saying where, or providing shoes for a person with no legs, or sailing without a compass.

The Need for a Common Good

It has been argued that character education does not require the religious principle of an afterlife in order to be successful. That might be true, but it does require a single common end. It requires at least an understanding of the common good of the civil community. But the very notion of a common good implies a common or shared meaning, that is, an end that is common.

Consider the common good of a hockey team. Victory is the end intended by the whole team, and every member of the team is working in conjunction with every other member to achieve that end, to be possessed by everyone as common property. A good scoring record (a means) is only good in view of the single and common end to be possessed by every member of the team, namely victory. A record with a high number of goals is good, because scoring many is necessary to realize the end. If there is a single end held in common that is larger than an individual good, then anyone who loves that common good over his own private good, such as his private scoring record, is a good and unselfish player.

Nevertheless, we have accepted the principle that at the heart of liberty is the right to define one's own concept of existence and of meaning. My concept of existence might not include a common good, rooted as it is in a common human nature and a common vision of that nature. With [Jean-Paul] Sartre, I might choose to regard myself as a "pour-soi" [for itself] without a nature, except the one I determine for myself by my absolutely free choices.

Perhaps we can give up the illusion that character education can bridge the gap between religious and nonreligious schools.

And if every player is allowed to decide what is the ultimate end without the franchise taking any definitive stand on what it is, then there is no common good to speak of, no criterion to determine what constitutes a good record, and thus no way to distinguish a good player from a bad one. A player who enters the rink without a stick and begins to perform quads and triple axels is just as good a player as one who plants himself on the blue line and shoots pucks into the seats, or one who stick handles by himself while skating backwards.

Character education might be a good idea, or it might very well be an insidious project that hides a nihilism that is too afraid or ashamed to rear its ugly head. It can do some good as long as the teacher has the good sense to ignore the nihilism lurking behind the postmodern liberalism that denies the very existence of universal truth and is willing to take a solid and realistic stand on what life is ultimately about and live it as a role model for students.

As a final point, Catholic educators can be thankful for not having to take on the absurd posture of having to teach the virtues in the hopes that students will have chosen the right end which alone makes them genuine virtues, but not being able to say what that end really is—not to mention that they are not to be called virtues, but "attributes." And perhaps we can give up the illusion that character education can bridge the gap between religious and nonreligious schools, as if there were now a common ground for a single system. There is no common ground if there is no shared vision, especially if such a moral and/or religious vision is forbidden from the start.

3

The Public School Setting Is Ideal for Teaching Ethics

Hannah McCrea

Hannah McCrea writes for The Seminal, an online community blog for independent media and politics.

Public school is the perfect venue for teaching ethics. The historical justification for public education itself also supports the teaching of values. The demand for ethics education among both public school teachers and members of the public is growing. Some teachers are already incorporating ethics into the curriculum, and a variety of materials are available for teachers to start teaching ethics. There are plenty of applications for ethics in the classroom within a variety of classes, including science, literature, and social studies. Teaching community ethics in public school would provide the commonality needed in an increasingly diverse society.

What's wrong with litter and road rage? What is the purpose of courtesy and respect when dealing with total strangers? Why is whistle-blowing and Samaritanism preferable to minding our own business? Why should we obey the law when we can get away with breaking it?

A Philosophy That Supports Ethics Education

Hopefully most of us have ready answers to these questions. However, spend a few weeks in virtually any American city and you'll learn that most Americans do not seem to have an-

Hannah McCrea, "Should Ethics Be Taught in Public Schools?" The Seminal, October 9, 2007. Reproduced by permission.

swers, or at least their answers differ significantly from mine. Public schools are the establishment best able to standardize our "learned" knowledge, beliefs, and behavior, and should therefore incorporate ethics into primary and secondary school curricula. Teaching ethics, either in distinct classes or by incorporating them into other areas of study, would provide schools and teachers with a forum for exposing, discussing, and applying "community ethics"—basic notions that we are all here and inherently equal, we are all members of a larger society, and we are all indeed in it together.

There is a difference between ethical guidance that presupposes the reason for acting a certain way . . . and that which offers good citizenship as the goal.

The historic reasoning behind free, universal, and compulsory education certainly supports an ethics curriculum. Even before the 19th century brought Horace Mann's "common school" movement, which was largely responsible for launching America's modern public education system, philosophers and progressive thinkers accepted the notion that in any true free society and participatory democracy the government has an obligation to educate its citizenry . . . to teach society's newest members to read, write, and compute, and to give them a basic understanding of their history, society, and the natural world in which they live, in order that they can access the democratic process and realize their own intellectual and productive potential.

As a diverse society founded on ideas of religious and economic freedom and equality, Americans exclude from this educational package any spiritual or moral instruction, an approach I generally support. But there is a difference between ethical guidance that presupposes the reason for acting a certain way (e.g., a higher power, a book of rules, an earthly mandate, etc.) and that which offers good citizenship as the goal. In this sense, teaching basic community ethics in schools upholds, rather than challenges, the fundamental reasons for having a universal, free, and compulsory education system.

Teachers Including Ethics

Anthony Tiatorio, an author and [a] 33-year veteran of the Mansfield, Massachusetts, public school system, is a long-time practitioner and advocate of teaching ethics in public schools. He has launched the Web site Ethics in Education [www.ethicsineducation.com], which provides a forum for teachers interested in including ethics in their curricula. The site "questions the wisdom of pursuing a virtues or character education model for teaching ethics and calls for a history-based, critical-thinking approach." Tiatorio writes of his experience trying to teach ethics in his secondary school social studies classes:

> Beginning with a provocative question intended to engage as many minds as possible, I asked: "Do you have any absolute obligation to others? Is there any scenario in which you must do good for at least one other person under at least some circumstances?" My students, nearly universally, said no! They did not recognize any responsibility to others of an absolute nature. So, I challenged them with increasingly more severe hypotheticals, probing for bottom: "You came upon a drowning man, a friend, a drowning child, your brother." Nothing penetrated the conviction that they were free spirits unfettered by any duty. . . . They would do it because they wanted to, not because they had to.

Following these experiences Tiatorio has written and amassed a body of material that he believes will assist teachers in providing their students with a useful ethics foundation. His collection of free workbooks and guides aim to help teachers discuss everything from Manifest Destiny to Hammurabi's Code from an ethics standpoint. He writes:

> To a large extent, ethical behavior, which is simply finding the balance between self-interest and group responsibility, is

largely, but not entirely, learned behavior standing in opposition to an instinct. . . . Not surprisingly then, many middle and high school students today will tell you that they themselves determine, as does every other individual, the standards of right and wrong. . . . Students must commit to broadening their own understanding of ethical issues by seeking to better understand the ideas of others. . . . It is necessary to build this into a sense of community within the class, and to encourage each student to participate energetically and cooperatively.

The applications of ethics teachings are abundant.

Tiatorio isn't the only one who considers the lack of ethical discussion in public schools a missed opportunity. Attorney Michael Sabbeth has been collaborating with Denver public schools since 1990 to incorporate ethics training into elementary school classes. The Institute for Global Ethics has also developed materials to help teachers include ethics in their curricula for grades K–5. These developments indicate a growing receptiveness, among both educators and normal citizens, toward including ethics training in the public education system.

Ethics Teachings

The applications of ethics teachings are abundant. For example, imagine the benefits of a widespread discussion of environmental ethics in public schools. How different would our children's collective sense of environmental stewardship be if they were all exposed to basic environmental concepts in conjunction with ethical notions of communal obligation and responsibility? (*Resources ARE scarce and finite. Humans DO have the ability to exhaust these resources and destroy their own environment beyond habitability. Who, then, is responsible for stopping this from happening?*)

25

How different would their sense of professional, political, and social integrity be if history and literature classes explored ethical questions of just cause, proportionality, intention, and authority? (*What was so "wrong" with invading Poland? Could [Fyodor] Dostoevsky's [Rodion Romanovich] Raskolnikov [a character in* Crime and Punishment*] have been me?*)

How better prepared would our children be for the medical or technological debates of the future if ideas behind freedom of choice, individual sovereignty, and sanctity of life were discussed in an open, frank manner in science class? (*Are we responsible for the consequences of our inventions? How can you justifiably control life-threatening overpopulation?*)

How would their outlook on crime and citizenship change if, when they were taught about government and democracy, they were challenged to consider what elements of right and wrong are legally codified, and why? (*Whom do laws serve, and why should I obey them? What right [do I] have to violate them or to try to change them? If something isn't illegal, why might it still be wrong?*) And so on.

It is precisely because [public] schools represent a distinct, nonfamilial, nonreligious setting that they are the ideal place for introducing community ethics.

Americans have historically opposed teaching ethics in schools, preferring to leave its discussion to families and religious establishments. We assume bringing ethics into public schools violates parents' rights to structure their children's moral upbringing themselves, or threatens the ideal that church and state should not only be separated in public schools, but that neither one religion nor secularism should be promoted at the expense of any other belief system.

However, it is precisely because schools represent a distinct, nonfamilial, nonreligious setting that they are the ideal place for introducing community ethics. Public schools are where students from different economic, racial, religious, and family backgrounds come together for conditioning that is common to all of us (excluding people educated in private schools) and thus represents a vital medium for instilling a standardized, collective, universal sense of society-wide ethics.

A society's collective sense of ethics affects its attitude toward everything from returning incorrect change to global warming. Yet, in a society as diverse and dynamic as ours, instilling any collective ethic will require that we harness the most universal form of public outreach: our public education system. Schools offer us the best means not only of offering our children knowledge, skills, and social conditioning, but [also] of encouraging their transformation into better, wiser, and more righteous players in a vast and ever-changing society.

4

Literature Is an Effective Tool for Character Education

Thomas Hibbs

Thomas Hibbs is a distinguished professor of ethics and culture and dean of the Honors College at Baylor University in Waco, Texas.

Stories, whether in print or in film, can serve an important role in moral education. In public school, character education is often a sham, but ways of incorporating character education without relying on it to do all the work of educating students about morals do exist. Classic literature, such as Jane Austen's Pride and Prejudice, *and newer literature, such as J.K. Rowling's Harry Potter books, can play an important role in developing the moral imagination. Even a story outdated in some ways can have much relevance to the young student dealing with his or her own contemporary moral dilemmas.*

"There are dark days ahead, Harry," says Dumbledore, Harry's mentor and the avuncular headmaster of Hogwarts [School of Witchcraft and Wizardry] . . . at the end of the recently released film *Harry Potter and the Goblet of Fire,* "days when we will be forced to choose between what is right and what is easy." One of the most magical things about J.K. Rowling's Harry Potter books and now films, the last two of which have been just splendid, is the way they subtly weave lessons about ethical choice and character into their gripping plots. Indeed, the plots themselves pivot on the crucial choices of the major characters for good or for evil, choices that at once form and reveal character.

Character Education in Schools

Attention to moments of choice and to the development of character, for example, in the latest Potter film and in the wonderful film version of Jane Austen's *Pride and Prejudice*, can help to educate the moral imagination of young and old alike. As Karen Bohlin, a senior scholar at the Center for the Advancement of Ethics and Character at Boston University, urges in her new book *Teaching Character Education Through Literature: Awakening the Moral Imagination in Secondary Classrooms*, the challenge for parents and educators is to "mitigate the range of negative narrative images and stimuli that feed the imaginations and aspirations of young people." The real danger in our culture is that many children grow up in a moral and spiritual vacuum into which the worst of Hollywood popular culture—film, music, and video games— marches to set up its own pedagogy, which atrophies the moral imagination and deforms desire.

Now, it is true that as practiced in many schools, character education is no more than a fad, deployed as a quick fix for rising violence, promiscuity, drug use, and incivility that afflict our youth. A scholar and secondary school administrator at Boston's Montrose School, Bohlin is acutely aware that much that passes for character education never transcends "simplistic slogans." Schools promote virtues the way Baskin-Robbins sells its flavor of the week, with posters of nice kids being nice to other nice kids. This is the sort of insubstantial rot through which young people see very quickly; it is, I would contend, one of the motives for rebellion among perceptive, slightly disaffected kids who yearn for something more than the latest superficial pitch from adults.

Of course, the very idea that the burden for character education would fall mainly upon schools is itself part of the problem. Except indirectly through its insistence upon responsible behavior and habits of hard work and truthfulness, schools aim primarily at the education of the intellect, not the passions of the heart. As Aristotle warned long ago, in matters ethical we must be wary of taking refuge in theory. We become virtuous not by thinking or arguing about virtue, but by doing, by the repetitious performance of virtuous acts. Aristotle compares education in virtue to the way in which we learn to play a musical instrument, become a competitive gymnast, or an excellent point guard.

The very idea that the burden for character education would fall mainly upon schools is itself part of the problem.

Awakening the Moral Imagination

But of course becoming virtuous involves more than rote, mindless action. It involves a cultivated moral imagination. This is precisely where Bohlin thinks schools can make a contribution to character education. Her book is a wonderful guide, both to the theory of character education and to the practical way in which literature—she offers explications [de texte] . . . for a number of novels including [F. Scott] Fitzgerald's *The Great Gatsby* and Austen's *Pride and Prejudice*—can serve to awaken the moral imagination.

Bohlin's treatment of *Pride and Prejudice* is deft and timely, with the release of the latest and perhaps finest film version of that marvelous novel. Indeed, both novel and film offer a corrective to an inordinately popular form of modern moral education—values clarification with its purported neutrality on the question of what is good. In the world of Jane Austen, ethics is largely about making judgments, about distinguishing between virtue and vice, between love and lust, between nobility and self-serving pride, between character and mere wealth or family lineage. In *Pride and Prejudice*, these issues play out most dramatically in the heart and mind of Elizabeth Bennet, whose confidence in her own superior judgment—and it is superior—is precisely what gets her into trouble. Her misjudgments are numerous and profound. As she comes to realize her multiple errors, she suffers "humiliation," but she has the good sense not to give up making judgments altogether, but to make an additional judgment that she now suffers a "just humiliation." The result is a development of Elizabeth's character, not in the direction of neutrality or mere toleration, but toward a greater imaginative sympathy with the range of character types, with an expanded sense of the rich variety of ways in which the good can be realized.

The neutrality of values clarification is always too late for virtue.

The Relevance for Students

One of the great advantages of Austen's fiction is that it gives the lie to our feigned classlessness. In our public morality, we talk endlessly about treating everyone equally and about the unimportance of *money* and possessions. But we make judgments all the time about money, income, looks, clothes, and possessions—nowhere more so than in our schools. Austen takes these matters seriously, but, since she takes virtue more seriously, she offers what we now lack, namely, a vocabulary for success and character. Despite its Victorian fascination with formality, Austen's world neatly dovetails with the world of contemporary teenagers. As Bohlin comments, "First impressions, battles of pride, the power of prejudice, pervasive gossip, and tensions between the genuine and the disingenuous in both friendship and romance are all quite real to" teenagers.

In fact, that's not a bad description of the boarding school social scene in *Harry Potter* [*and the Goblet of Fire*]. Critics have been agog about the latest installment being more adult, by which many seem to mean that hormones now figure importantly in the lives of Harry, Ron, and Hermione. But this only serves to heighten the significance of friendship, fidelity, truthfulness, and courage, on the one hand, and betrayal, disloyalty, deception, and cowardice, on the other. The latest film repeatedly makes an important point about the nature of courage. In the latest story, Harry is increasingly isolated, facing burdens that only he can bear even as he suffers the skeptical taunts of others, the suspicions of friends, and even self-doubt. In the midst of this, he is forced into direct confrontations with evil against [which] he must leverage enormous skill and courage. Voldemort, Harry's demonic nemesis, specializes in what appears to be courage: the powerful overcoming of obstacles and the ability to do without flinching what others fear. But if, as is true of Voldemort, we separate valor from the common good, from justice and friendship, then we are left with nihilism, the empty expression of power for its own sake—a position advocated explicitly by Voldemort in the first film.

To Voldemort's duplicitous fearmongering and intimidation, Dumbledore proposes truthfulness about the evils the children at his school will soon face. He also stresses the need for "fierce friendship," accountability to others, and a willingness to sacrifice one's life for the common good. In the world of Harry Potter or Elizabeth Bennet, as in our world, the neutrality of values clarification is always too late for virtue.

5

Public Schools That Teach Character Help Close the Achievement Gap

David Whitman

David Whitman is a journalist and the author of Sweating the Small Stuff: Inner-City Schools and the New Paternalism.

Paternalistic schools offer a promising model for closing the achievement gap between white and minority students. These schools not only stress academics, but also stress character development and the development of virtues. Such an emphasis on both academics and character has the result of replacing street culture with a culture of achievement. The paternalism at such schools is a gentle paternalism that both liberals and conservatives can embrace, for different reasons. Despite how well these schools are working, implementing more of them remains a challenge, mainly due to the reluctance to accept the key elements of such schools.

By the time youngsters reach high school in the United States, the achievement gap is immense. The average black 12th grader has the reading and writing skills of a typical white 8th grader and the math skills of a typical white 7th grader. The gap between white and Hispanic students is similar. But some remarkable inner-city schools are showing that the achievement gap can be closed, even at the middle and high school level, if poor minority kids are given the right kind of instruction.

David Whitman, "An Appeal to Authority: The New Paternalism in Urban Schools," *Education Next*, vol. 8, no. 4, Fall 2008, pp. 53–58. Copyright © 2008 by the Board of Trustees of Leland Stanford Junior University. Reproduced by permission.

Paternalistic Schools

Over the past two years, I have visited six outstanding schools. All of these educational gems enroll minority youngsters from rough urban neighborhoods with initially poor to mediocre academic skills; all but one are open-admission schools that admit students mostly by lottery. Their middle school students perform as well as their white peers, and in some middle schools, minority students learn at a rate comparable to that of affluent white students in their state's top schools. At the high school level, low-income minority students are more likely to matriculate to college than their more advantaged peers, with more than 95 percent of graduates gaining admission to college. Not surprisingly, they all have gifted, deeply committed teachers and dedicated, forceful principals. They also have rigorous academic standards, test students frequently, and carefully monitor students' academic performance to assess where students need help. "Accountability," for both teachers and students, is not a loaded code word but a lodestar. Students take a college-prep curriculum and are not tracked into vocational or noncollege-bound classes. Most of the schools have uniforms or a dress code, an extended school day, and three weeks of summer school.

Yet above all, these schools share a trait that has been largely ignored by education researchers: They are *paternalistic* institutions. By paternalistic I mean that each of the six schools is a highly prescriptive institution that teaches students not just how to think, but also how to act according to what are commonly termed traditional, middle-class values. These paternalistic schools go beyond just teaching values as abstractions: The schools tell students exactly how they are expected to behave, and their behavior is closely monitored, with real rewards for compliance and penalties for noncompliance. Unlike the often-forbidding paternalistic institutions of the past, these schools are prescriptive yet warm; teachers and principals, who sometimes serve in loco parentis [in the place of a parent], are both authoritative and caring figures. Teachers laugh with and cajole students, in addition to frequently directing them to stay on task.

The new breed of paternalistic schools appears to be the single most effective way of closing the achievement gap. No other school model or policy reform in urban secondary schools seems to come close to having such a dramatic impact on the performance of inner-city students. Done right, paternalistic schooling provides a novel way to remake inner-city education in the years ahead.

But while these "no excuses" schools have demonstrated remarkable results, the notion of reintroducing paternalism in inner-city schools is deeply at odds with the conventional wisdom of the K–12 education establishment. For a host of reasons, teachers' unions, school board members, ed school professors, big-city school administrators, multicultural activists, bilingual educators, and progressive-education proponents do not embrace the idea that what might most help disadvantaged students are highly prescriptive schools that favor traditional instructional methods. And even the many parents who are foursquare in favor of what paternalistic schools do cringe at labeling the schools in those terms. In 2008, "paternalism" remains a dirty word in American culture.

Paternalistic schools go beyond just teaching values as abstractions.

Paternalism Reborn

What is paternalism and why does it have so few friends? Webster's [dictionary] defines paternalism as a principle or system of governing that echoes a father's relationship with his children. Paternalistic policies interfere with the freedom of individuals, and this interference is justified by the argument that the individuals will be better off as a result. Paternalism is controversial because it contains an element of moral arrogance, an assertion of superior competence. But in the last decade, government paternalism has enjoyed a kind of rebirth.

In a 1997 volume titled *The New Paternalism[: Supervisory Approaches to Poverty]*, New York University professor Lawrence Mead, the leading revisionist, explored the emergence of a new breed of paternalistic policies aimed at reducing poverty, welfare dependency, and other social problems by closely supervising the poor. These paternalistic programs try to curb social problems by imposing behavioral requirements for assistance and then monitoring recipients to ensure compliance. "Misbehavior is not just punished" in paternalistic programs, writes Mead. "It is *preempted* by the oversight of authority figures, much as parents supervise their families." The schools I visited are paternalistic in the very way Mead describes.

Paternalistic programs survive only because they typically enforce values that "clients already believe," Mead notes. But many paternalistic programs remain controversial because they seek to change the lifestyles of the poor, immigrants, and minorities, rather than the lifestyles of middle-class and upper-class families. The paternalistic presumption implicit in the schools is that the poor lack the family and community support, cultural capital, and personal follow-through to live according to the middle-class values that they, too, espouse.

In the narrowest sense, all American schools are paternalistic. "Schooling virtually defines what paternalism means in a democratic society," the political scientist James Q. Wilson has written. Elementary schools often attempt to teach values and enforce rules about how students are to behave and treat others. The truth is that hundreds of parochial and traditional public schools in the inner city are authoritarian institutions with pronounced paternalistic elements. Yet the new paternalistic schools I visited look and feel very different from these more commonplace institutions.

Curbing Disorder

The most distinctive feature of new paternalistic schools is that they are fixated on curbing disorder. The emphasis springs from an understanding of urban schools that owes much to James Q. Wilson and George L. Kelling's well-known "broken windows" theory of crime reduction: The idea that disorder and even *signs* of disorder (e.g., the broken window left unfixed) are the fatal undoing of urban neighborhoods. That is why these schools devote inordinate attention to making sure that shirts are tucked in, bathrooms are kept clean, students speak politely, and trash is picked up.

Paternalistic schools teach character and middle-class virtues like diligence, politeness, cleanliness, and thrift. They impose detentions for tardiness and disruptive behavior in class and forbid pupils from cursing at or talking disrespectfully to teachers. But the new paternalistic schools go further than even strict Catholic schools in prescribing student conduct and minimizing signs of disorder.

Pupils are typically taught not just to walk rather than run in the hallway—they learn *how* to walk from class to class: silently, with a book in hand. In class, teachers constantly monitor whether students are tracking them with their eyes, whether students nod their heads to show that they are listening, and if students have slouched in their seats. Amistad Academy enforces a zero-tolerance policy. Calling out in class, distracting other students, rolling your eyes at a teacher—all rather common occurrences in most middle-school classrooms—result in students being sent to a "time out" desk or losing "scholar dollars" from virtual "paychecks" that can be used to earn special privileges at school.

Teachers ceaselessly monitor student conduct and character development to assess if students are acting respectfully, developing self-discipline, displaying good manners, working hard, and taking responsibility for their actions. The SEED School [a public boarding school in Washington, D.C.] even requires students to have teachers sign a note after each class assessing how the student performed on a list of 12 "responsible behaviors" and 12 "irresponsible behaviors."

Paternalistic schools teach character and middle-class virtues like diligence, politeness, cleanliness, and thrift.

Culture Change

Paternalistic schools are culturally authoritative schools as well. Their pupils learn—and practice—how to shake hands when they are introduced to someone. At SEED and Cristo Rey [Jesuit High School in Chicago, IL], students practice sitting down to a formal place setting typical of a restaurant and learn the difference between the dinner fork and the salad fork. The new paternalistic schools thus build up the "cultural capital" of low-income students by taking them to concerts, to Shakespearean plays, on trips to Washington, D.C., and to national parks. They help students find white-collar internships, and teach them how to comport themselves in an office.

One of the distinctive features of Cristo Rey is its novel work-study program, which dispatches students one day a week to clerical jobs in downtown Chicago in accounting firms, banks, insurance companies, law firms, and offices of health care providers. For the first time in their lives, students are surrounded by white-collar professionals who had to attend college and graduate schools as a prerequisite to landing their jobs.

At the same time that these schools reinforce middle-class mores, they also steadfastly suppress all aspects of street culture. Street slang, the use of the "n-word," and cursing are typically barred not only in the classroom but in hallways and lunchrooms as well. Merely fraternizing with gang members can lead to expulsion. If students so much as doodle gang graffiti on a notebook or a piece of paper at Cristo Rey, they are suspended. And if they doodle a gang symbol a second time, Principal Pat Garrity expels them. The school day and year are extended in part to boost academic achievement, but also to keep kids off the street and out of homes with few academic supports.

The prescriptive rigor and accountability of paternalistic schools extend not just to student character and conduct but to academics as well. AIPCS [American Indian Public Charter School] is one of only two middle schools in Oakland [California] to require every 8th grader—including special ed students—to take Algebra I. All KIPP [Knowledge Is Power Program] Academy [in South Bronx, New York] 8th graders complete a two-year high school–level Algebra I course and take the New York State Math A Regents exam, a high school exit exam. In 2006, an astonishing 85 percent passed it.

By their very nature, the new paternalistic schools for teens tend to displace a piece of parents' traditional role in transmitting values.

A Culture of Achievement

Paternalistic schools, in short, push *all* students to perform to high standards. They spell out exactly what their pupils are supposed to learn and then ride herd on them until they master it. From the first day students walk through the door, their principal and teachers envelop them in a college-going ethos, with the goal that 100 percent of students will be admitted into college. Over time, paternalistic schools create a culture of achievement that is the antithesis of street culture.

By their very nature, the new paternalistic schools for teens tend to displace a piece of parents' traditional role in transmitting values. Most of the schools are founded on the premise that minority parents want to do the right thing but often don't have the time or resources to keep their children from being dragged down by an unhealthy street culture. But the schools do not presume that boosting parental participation is the key to narrowing the achievement gap. Parents' chief role at no-excuses schools is helping to steer their children through the door—paternalistic schools are typically schools of choice—and then ensuring that their children get to school on time.

Principals and teachers at these schools are surprisingly familiar with students' personal lives. As a result, students call on teachers and principals for advice and help. Teachers are deeply devoted to their students, often answering phone queries from students late into the night, showing up before school starts to help a struggling pupil, or staying late to help tutor. A KIPP student recalls, "I needed help in math in 5th grade and called my teacher one week three times a night." It is not uncommon for students to describe their schools as a "second home."

What really makes this a kinder, gentler form of paternalism is that parents, typically single mothers, choose to send their children to these inner-city schools—but they are also acting under duress. They believe their neighborhood schools fail to educate students and are breeding grounds for gang strife and drugs. They are often desperate for alternatives, and are particularly excited to find a no-nonsense public school committed to readying their children for college. In this sense, paternalistic schools draw a self-selected student population. Even so, there is surprisingly little evidence that these schools are "creaming" the best and brightest minority students. At most of these schools, students are typically one to two grade levels behind their age-level peers when they arrive. . . .

Paternalistic Schools Appeal to Liberals and Conservatives

As Lawrence Mead has pointed out, paternalism is neither conservative nor liberal per se; in some eras of American history, liberals have pressed for paternalistic programs, while at other times conservatives have lobbied for them. At first glance, the character training and rituals of these paternalistic schools give them a decidedly traditional feel. The schools teach old-fashioned virtues, simply put. Yet these virtues— perseverance, discipline, politeness—are really the same as the "noncognitive skills" that liberal education reformers like Richard Rothstein and economists like James Heckman want inner-city schools to boost in order to raise academic achievement and compensate for low-income students' economic and cultural deficits.

In fact, the founders of many of today's paternalistic schools are liberals who believe that closing the pernicious achievement gulf between white and minority students is the central civil rights issue of our century. Most of the founders and principals of the schools I visited were uneasy with having their schools described as paternalistic. "I don't think there is a positive way to say a school is paternalistic," Eric Adler, cofounder of the SEED School in Washington, D.C., asserted. Dave Levin, cofounder of the network of KIPP schools, shared Adler's reservations: "To say that a school is paternalistic suggests that we are condescending, rather than serving in the role of additional parents. . . ."

Today's paternalistic schools are more palatable to liberals than earlier models were because their curricula for character development promote not only traditional virtues but also social activism. SEED, for example, explicitly encourages community involvement in progressive causes, as do KIPP Academy, Cristo Rey, and University Park [Campus School, Worcester, Massachusetts]. SEED requires students to participate in community service projects and teaches each student to "make a commitment to a life of social action." Students are urged to reflect on their own experiences with prejudice, discrimination, and bullying.

While liberals applaud these schools for placing poor kids on the path toward college (and out of poverty), conservatives cheer them for teaching the work ethic and traditional virtues. And there is great demand for seats in paternalistic schools among inner-city parents. So why not create lots more of them? Unfortunately, the three legs of the education establishment tripod—teachers' unions, the district bureaucracy, and education schools—are all unlikely to embrace key elements that make paternalistic schools work.

Today's paternalistic schools are more palatable to liberals ... because their curricula for character development promote not only traditional virtues but also social activism.

Key Elements of Paternalistic Schools

In paternalistic schools, principals must be able to assemble teams of teachers with a personal commitment to closing the achievement gap, teachers who are willing to work an extended school day and school year, who want to instruct teens about both traditional course matter and character development, and who will make themselves available to students as needed. But requiring teachers to work longer days and years would in most cases violate union contracts. So would allowing principals to handpick teachers (who may or may not be certified) and fire those who are not successful in the classroom. District bureaucrats, meanwhile, are loath to grant individual schools the freedom to do things differently, especially when it comes to curriculum and budget.

It would appear that education schools (and many K–12 educators trained there) bear a special animosity toward paternalism and its instructional incarnations. This is evident in their dislike of teacher-directed instruction, "drill-and-kill" memorization, rote learning, and direct instructional methods that emphasize the importance of acquiring basic facts and skills.

The romantic educational philosophy of Jean-Jacques Rousseau (and his American heir, John Dewey) continues to prevail. Most K–12 educators (and their teachers in ed schools) believe students should be free to explore, to cultivate a love of learning, and to develop their "critical thinking" skills unencumbered by rote learning. By contrast, the new paternalistic schools are animated more by obligation than freedom. Mead argues that "the problem of poverty or underachievement is not that the poor lack freedom. The real problem is that the poor are *too* free." Paternalistic schools assume that disadvantaged students do best when structure and expectations are crystal clear, rather than presuming that kids should learn to figure things out for themselves.

District bureaucrats . . . are loath to grant individual schools the freedom to do things differently, especially when it comes to curriculum and budget.

Were it not for the recalcitrance of the education establishment, a grand bargain might be in the offing: If inner-city schools across the nation successfully adopted a no-excuses model, perhaps conservatives would be willing to support spending increases for longer school days, an extended school year, and additional tutoring. And perhaps liberals would be willing to grant principals and teachers of these schools a great deal of autonomy, allowing these schools to circumvent state and district regulations and union contracts.

For now, the spread of paternalistic schooling is taking place on a school-by-school basis in dozens of schools, but not on a massive scale. Unlike earlier generations of exemplary inner-city schools, today's paternalistic institutions fortunately follow replicable school models and do not depend heavily on charismatic principals whose leadership cannot be copied elsewhere. The founders of these schools are devoting substantial resources to replicating their flagship schools, but they continue to encounter obstacles both political and practical. The difficulty of funding an extended school day and year, the reluctance of districts to grant autonomy to innovative school leaders, and the flawed charter laws and union contracts that tie the hands of entrepreneurs are just some of the factors that impede the spread of paternalistic reform. These obstacles make the restructuring of inner-city schools en masse in the mold of paternalism unlikely in the near future.

Still, these entrepreneurial school founders battle on, slowly replicating their institutions across the country. It is too soon to say that all of the copycat schools will succeed. But the early results are extremely encouraging. It is possible that these schools, so radically different from traditional public schools, could one day educate not just several thousand inner-city youngsters but tens or even hundreds of thousands of students in cities across the nation. Done well, paternalistic schooling would constitute a major stride toward reducing the achievement gap and the lingering disgrace of racial inequality in urban America.

6

Public Schools Indoctrinate Students and Don't Reflect the Majority's Values

Phyllis Schlafly

Phyllis Schlafly is an attorney and the author of The Suprema-cists: The Tyranny of Judges and How to Stop It.

Public schools have more influence on directing culture than any other arm of government. Public schools have always played a role in defining culture, and the schools used to pass on objective values informed by religion and patriotism. Public schools since the 1960s have rejected objective values and have started to pass on a system of values in which anything goes. This style of education that is supposedly neutral on values actually ends up in-doctrinating students with values that are in direct opposition to what their parents want.

With all the public discussion about whether values vot-ers would vote in the 2006 election or stay home, the underlying and still unanswered question is, what is the role of government in defining our culture?

Do both red states and blue states look to government to set or guide our cultural direction, whether it is about mar-riage versus the gay agenda, free speech versus pornography, life versus abortion/cloning/euthanasia, property rights versus community development, or sovereignty/patriotism versus globalism/open borders?

Phyllis Schlafly, "Like It or Not, Public Schools Define American Culture," Town-hall.com, November 14, 2006. Reproduced by permission of the author.

Do we believe in a very limited government that would allow all these issues to be thrashed out and decided by big media, special interest groups, and 527 unregulated political action committees? Should we demand that our elected representatives pass laws to address these issues, or should we allow appointed judges to make those policy decisions for us?

Laws, judicial decisions and media have a powerful effect on our culture.

But more influential than all those in directing our culture is the arm of government known as the public schools.

The Historical Role of Public Schools

Public schools are guiding the morals, attitudes, knowledge and decision making (the elements that determine our culture) of 89 percent of U.S. children. Public schools are financed by $500 billion a year of our money, forcibly taken from us in taxes, which the public school establishment spends under a thin veneer of accountability to school board members elected in government-run elections.

Quo vadis [where are you going]? Whither are the public schools taking the next generation?

Public schools are guiding the morals, attitudes, knowledge and decision making (the elements that determine our culture) of 89 percent of U.S. children.

Prior to the 1960s, public schools and teachers clearly accepted their role in defining the culture of the youngsters under their supervision. The public schools, using a McGuffey Reader–style curriculum, were the mechanism through which U.S. children learned not only the basics but also values such as honesty and patriotism, and immigrant children assimilated by learning our language, laws and customs.

The American Citizens Handbook, published for teachers by the National Education Association in 1951, proclaimed:

"It is important that people who are to live and work together shall have a common mind—a like heritage of purpose, religious ideals, love of country, beauty, and wisdom to guide and inspire them." This message was fortified by selections suitable for memorization, such as Old and New Testament passages, the Ten Commandments, the Lord's Prayer, the Golden Rule, the Boy Scout oath, and patriotic songs.

The turning point in public schools came in the 1960s with the vast influence of the humanist John Dewey and his Columbia [University] Teachers College acolytes, who argued against objective truth, authoritative notions of good and evil, religion and tradition. Sidney Simon's 1972 book *Values Clarification*, which sold nearly 1 million copies, was widely used to teach students to "clarify" their values, i.e., cast off their parents' values and make their own choices based on situation ethics.

Then the public schools welcomed the [Alfred] Kinsey-trained experts to change the sexual mores of our society from favoring sex-in-marriage to diversity. Concepts of right and wrong were banished, and children were taught about varieties of sex without reference to what is moral, good or even legal.

Meanwhile, the curriculum suffered a vast dumbing down, allowing students to graduate without learning to read or calculate. U.S. history courses now inculcate the doctrines of U.S. guilt and multiculturalism instead of the greatness of our heroes and successes.

Schools Defining Culture

By the 1990s, public schools effectively adopted a modis operandi [method of operating] described by U.S. Sen. Hillary Clinton, D-N.Y., as the village should raise the child. Public schools have become fortresses in which administrators exercise near-absolute power to determine the student values, morals, attitudes and hopes, while parents are kept outside the barricades.

Using activist judges to shore up their monopoly power, the schools persuaded the 9th U.S. Circuit Court of Appeals to rule last year [2005] that a public school can teach students "whatever information it wishes to provide, sexual or otherwise," and that parents' rights to control the upbringing of their children "does not extend beyond the threshold of the school door."

Government schools are every day defining the culture of the nation our children will live in, and they are doing it in violation of what the American people want.

After heavy criticism in the U.S. House of Representatives, the court reaffirmed its decision but tried to soften the "threshold" sentence.

The meaning of "whatever" is spelled out in anti-parent, pro–public school decisions handed down in five circuits within the last two years. Federal courts upheld the right of public schools to indoctrinate students in Muslim religion and practices, to force students to watch a one-hour pro-homosexual video, to censor any mention of intelligent design, to use classroom materials that parents consider pornographic, to force students to answer nosy questionnaires with suggestive questions about sex and suicide, and to prohibit antigay T-shirts but welcome anti-Bush T-shirts.

It's not a question of whether, or if, government should define our culture. Government schools are every day defining the culture of the nation our children will live in, and they are doing it in violation of what the American people want.

7

Public Schools Must Revive Moral Education

William Damon

William Damon is a professor of education at Stanford University, the director of the Stanford Center on Adolescence, and a senior fellow at the Hoover Institution. He is the author of Bringing in a New Era in Character Education.

Although people still question whether character education should or should not be a part of public schooling, the reality is that public schools inevitably engage in character education. Given that this moral education is inescapable, schools need to focus on doing a good job of it. One of the current trends in character education that focuses on children's self-esteem and subjective feelings constitutes a failed model for passing on morals. What is needed is an understanding of the rich moral traditions found in every culture and religion. Using these traditions as support for principles of ethics allows educators to engage in character education in a manner that appeals to objective standards that reveal truths about human nature.

It is an odd mark of our time that the first question people ask about character education is whether public schools should be doing it at all. The question is odd because it invites us to imagine that schooling, which occupies about a third of a child's waking time, somehow could be arranged to play no role in the formation of a child's character.

William Damon, "Good? Bad? or None of the Above? The Time-Honored, Unavoidable Mandate to Teach Character," *Education Next*, vol. 5, no. 2, Spring 2005, pp. 21, 24–27. Copyright © 2005 by the Board of Trustees of Leland Stanford Junior University. Reproduced by permission.

Try to imagine a school that did manage to stay out of the character education business, refraining from promoting virtues such as honesty and respectfulness. Even if the school survived the chaos that would ensue, could we expect that the character of its students wouldn't be affected (adversely, in this case) by the message that such an abdication of responsibility would impart? For better or worse, every school envelops its students in a moral climate. The choices that the school makes—or fails to make—about what sort of moral climate to create inevitably leave lasting marks on the students who live and learn there. Moral education, in the title phrase of one early book on the matter, "comes with the territory." . . .

The Inner-Directed Society

Whether, not how, to educate for character . . . remains essentially unanswered, a condition that creates doubt and debate among educators and the public. Far from worrying about how to preserve children's autonomy, however, skeptics now complain that character education is not forceful enough in presenting children with the stark and incontestable contrast between right and wrong. In a recent book, with the perhaps understandably overwrought title *The Death of Character: Moral Education in an Age Without Good or Evil,* James Davison Hunter criticizes character education for its failure to promote morality with sufficient strength and clarity. The problem, according to Hunter, a professor of sociology and religion at the University of Virginia, lies in the psychologically oriented pedagogy that character educators turn to in teaching values to children: "Dominated as it is by perspectives diffused and diluted from professional psychology, this regime is overwhelmingly therapeutic and self-referencing; in character, its defining feature is a moral framework whose center point is the autonomous self." By focusing on the child's everyday behavior and feelings, moral values get watered down and lost.

Indeed, a recent research review by Marvin [W.] Berkowitz and Melinda Bier of the University of Missouri (at St. Louis) found that the most common topic in today's character education programs is "social-emotional content"—in particular, what they call "personal improvement/self-management and awareness (self-control, goal setting, relaxation techniques, self-awareness, emotional awareness)." Exactly what part of a child's moral development might be stimulated by relaxation or emotional awareness training is a mystery that neither science nor philosophy has shed much light on. My guess is that such feeling states have little to do with the acquisition of childhood morality and that, as Hunter complains, a pedagogy built primarily around the self's sentiments may distract children from the real challenges of forging character.

When the drive to boost children's self-esteem interferes with moral instruction, it goes beyond silly to harmful.

The Right, the Wrong, and the Strictly Instrumental

The contemporary character-education movement has thus been misled by the trendy notion that children's positive feelings are the key to all sorts of learning, moral as well as academic. Many educators now engage in silly activities and exercises focused on an obsessive attention to children's self-esteem, a focus that has foisted warehouses' worth of nonsense on students. (One assignment given my youngest daughter in her elementary school days was to write, "I'm terrific," 20 times on a 3x5 card—which she dutifully did, all the while wondering aloud what in fact she was terrific at.) When the drive to boost children's self-esteem interferes with moral instruction, it goes beyond silly to harmful.

Once when I was a guest on a National Public Radio show, a parent of a 5th-grade student called in to discuss an incident that was highly upsetting to her but all too familiar to me. That week her son had been sent home with a note informing her that he had been caught taking money out of fellow students' backpacks. The mother quickly got on the phone to the boy's teacher to tell her she was appalled, that she couldn't bear the thought of her son stealing from his friends. "What can we do about this?" asked the mother. To her astonishment, the teacher responded by asking her to say and do nothing. "We were obliged to inform you of what happened," the teacher said, "but now we wish to handle this in our own professional way. And to start with, we are not calling this incident 'stealing.' That would just give your child a bad self-image. We've decided to call what your son did 'uncooperative behavior'—and we'll point out to him in no uncertain terms that he won't be very popular with his friends if he keeps acting this way!" The parent reported that the boy now ignored her efforts to counsel him about the matter. She worried that he had "blown the whole thing off" without learning anything from it at all.

In its "professional" judgments, the school had translated a wrongful act (stealing) into a strictly instrumental concern (losing popularity). The school did so in order to save the child from feelings (shame, guilt) that it assumed could cause the child discomfort and thereby damage the child's self-image. The school was right on the first count and mistaken on the second. The child probably would have felt embarrassed if forcefully told that he had committed a moral offense—and such an experience in firsthand shame and guilt is precisely what researchers have found to be a primary means of moral learning. There is no credible scientific evidence that supports the idea that a child's self-image can be harmed by reprimands for wrongdoing, as long as the feedback pertains to the behavior rather than to the child's own intrinsic self-worth.

Confusing Ourselves and Our Students

Over the years I have often been asked to help resolve trouble in schools torn apart by cheating scandals. In each case, the resistance of teachers to discussing the moral meaning of the incident with students was palpable. I explain to them that the moral issues are many, but by no means hard to understand. Cheating is wrong for at least four reasons: it gives students who cheat an unfair advantage over those who do not cheat; it is dishonest; it is a violation of trust; and it undermines the academic integrity, the code of conduct, and the social order of the school.

I am still shocked at the number of teachers who say, in front of their students, that it is hard to hold students to a no-cheating standard in a society where people cheat on taxes, on their spouses, and so on. Some teachers sympathize with student cheaters because they think that the tests students take are flawed or unfair. Some pardon students because they believe that sharing schoolwork is motivated by loyalty to friends. In my experience, it can take days of intense discussion, and some arm twisting, to get a school community to develop a no-cheating standard that is solidly supported by expressions of moral concern.

In our time, a hesitancy to use a moral language remains the most stubborn and distracting problem for character education. Teachers worry that words that shame children may wound their self-esteem; that there are no words of moral truth anyway; that it is hypocritical to preach moral codes to the young when so many adults ignore them; or that in a diverse society one person's moral truth is another's moral falsehood. Yet adult expressions of clear moral standards are precisely what guide character formation in the young.

The conviction that moral standards are not arbitrary, that they reflect basic human truths and therefore that they must be passed from generation to generation is a necessary prerequisite of all moral education. This was a point that sociologist

Émile Durkheim made in his great 1902–03 lectures, "Moral Education," the foundation for most modern approaches to the subject. Even those who started their moral education work from a different direction, such as Harvard psychologist Lawrence Kohlberg, came around to this view once they tried their hand at the actual practice of teaching children good values.

In our time, a hesitancy to use a moral language remains the most stubborn and distracting problem for character education.

The Need for Objective Standards

The contours of what we must do are clear: Public schools must accept the mandate of educating for character. Since they shape student character no matter what they do, schools may as well try to do a good job at it. Schools must present students with objective standards expressed in a moral language that sharply distinguishes right from wrong and directs students to behave accordingly. Sentiments such as "feeling better" cannot stand as sufficient reason for moral choice. A school must help students understand that they are expected to be honest, fair, compassionate, and respectful whether it makes them feel good or not. The character mandate that adults must pass on to children transcends time, place, or personal feelings.

The cauldron of day-to-day practice, of course, always contains a steamy mixture of disparate elements. What schools actually do with character education cannot be summed up in one easy generalization. At the classroom level, education is a pragmatic, seat-of-the-pants enterprise in which teachers tend to throw whatever they have at students, and character educators are no exception.

For clues about what we can do, let us return for a moment to the James [Davison] Hunter critique quoted earlier. The complaint was that character education "in a time without good or evil" provides children with the following moral logic: To the question "Why should one not be bad, say, through stealing or cheating?" follows the reply, "How would it make you feel if someone did that to you?" As I suggested earlier, Hunter is correct that the moral logic here is not sufficient, because stealing or cheating is wrong no matter how anyone feels about it. But Hunter's complaint is too sweeping and in its overreach misses a valuable opportunity to educate children about the foundations of moral behavior and belief.

Since they shape student character no matter what they do, schools may as well try to do a good job at it.

The Golden Rule

Suppose that the teacher took the response, "How would it make you feel if someone did that to you?" an extra step—backward through the ages of moral tradition—linking what Hunter takes to be a mere touchy-feely sentiment to one of the great moral maxims of all time: the Golden Rule. The version most familiar in Western society—"Do unto others as you would have them do unto you"—is in fact a general precept shared by most of the world's religions. While asking the child to take the perspective of another who would be hurt by a harmful act, a teacher could draw the student's attention to the great moral traditions that have proclaimed the importance of doing so, connecting the student's personal sentiments with the earlier wisdom of civilizations. The teacher could introduce students to the glorious panoply of worldwide philosophical thought that has celebrated this principle. A lively classroom discussion could ensue from exploring why so much profound thinking across so many diverse times and places has focused on this classic maxim.

Pointing out the rich religious and historical traditions behind a maxim underlines its deep importance in human life. It informs students of the universal and timeless truths underlying moral strictures. It does not imply proselytizing for a particular religious doctrine, because the universality of core moral principles can be easily demonstrated. This kind of instruction is needed pedagogically not only because it elicits historical interest, but also because it adds a dimension of moral gravity and objectivity to what otherwise would stand only as a simple statement of a child's personal feelings.

If a child's moral education is limited to stimulating self-reflection about his personal feelings, not much has been accomplished. But if the child's moral education begins with a consideration of moral feelings such as empathy and then links these feelings with the enduring elements of morality, the child's character growth will be enhanced by transforming the child's emotions—which do play a key role in behavior—into a lasting set of virtues.

An essential part of moral education is reaffirming the emotional sense of moral regret that young people naturally feel when they harm another person or violate a fundamental societal standard. Every child is born with a capacity to feel empathy for a person who is harmed, with a capacity to feel outrage when a social standard is violated, and with a capacity to feel shame or guilt for doing something wrong. This is a natural, emotional basis for character development, but it quickly atrophies without the right kinds of feedback—in particular, guidance that supports the moral sense and shows how it can be applied to the range of social concerns that one encounters in human affairs. A primary way that schools can provide students with this kind of guidance is to teach them the great traditions that have endowed us with our moral standards.

The Golden Rule is a prototypical moral maxim with both a long historical legacy and widely recognized contemporary usefulness. (It is explicitly taught and practiced in the field of business management, a fact that many high school students would very likely be interested to learn.) There are legions of maxims in the living lore of our common culture, and many, like the Golden Rule, bear a moral message: "Two wrongs don't make a right" (ancient Scots); "You are only as good as your word" (early American); "Honesty is the best policy" ([Miguel de]Cervantes, Ben Franklin); "It's better to light a single candle than to curse the darkness" (old Chinese proverb). As education policy maker Arthur Schwartz has written, each of these "wise sayings" encapsulates a store of wisdom that has been handed down to us through countless conversations across the generations.

Our Moral Traditions

What these ancient maxims suggest is that societies distant from us in time and place have something important to tell us regarding our efforts to educate young people for character. Among other things, they remind us that neither we nor our children need to invent civilization from scratch. Our journeys in moral learning begin with the aid of our rich cultural traditions and the living wisdom found therein. We are inheritors of a wealth of moral knowledge, a set of universal truths drawn from the forge of human experience over the centuries. In our transient lifestyles and throw-away relationships, in our modernist commitment to the autonomous self, we sometimes forget this. But in our role as guardians of the young, we must share the obligation to pass on to our children that which civilization has given us.

All this, of course, flies in the face of "constructivist" approaches to education favored in recent decades. Supposedly, children learn nothing useful through memorization; and, we have been warned, rote learning leads only to boredom and rejection, going "in one ear and out the other." But as I have written elsewhere, such fears are simplistic as well as unsupported by evidence. The contrast between the "discovery learning" of constructivism and the practice-and-drill of traditional learning is a false opposition. Children benefit from both, they require both, and the two complement rather than fight each other in the actual dynamics of mastering knowledge. The usefulness of memorized bits of wisdom that are stored away and used at later times, when they are better understood in the light of lived experience, has been fully supported by developmental theories ranging from the social-cultural to the biological.

We do not invent our ethical codes from scratch, nor should we expect that our children could.

One of the other principles of psychological development is that children learn best when they confront clear and consistent messages in numerous ways and in multiple contexts. In the character arena, young people need to hear moral messages from all the respected people in their lives if they are to take the messages to heart. A student learns honesty in a deep and lasting way when a teacher explains why cheating undermines the academic mission, when a parent demonstrates the importance of telling the truth for family solidarity, when a sports coach discourages deceit because it defeats the purpose of fair competition, and when a friend shows why lies destroy the trust necessary for a close relationship. The student then acquires a sense of why honesty is important to all the human relationships that the student will participate in, now and in the future.

And the past plays a part in moral learning. We do not invent our ethical codes from scratch, nor should we expect that our children could. Our inherited moral traditions are the essential elements of civilized society. When presented to students through a lively pedagogy of received wisdom, such as may be found in common maxims and precepts, these moral

traditions can provide a compelling historical dimension to character education. For too long our public schools have hidden away the historical dimension, keeping the traditional foundations of moral instruction out of sight. It is time to remove this unnecessary handicap and build the moral futures of our children on the best wisdom that the past and present can offer.

8

Public Schools Are the Source of the Decline in Morality Among Teens

David N. Bass

David N. Bass is an investigative reporter and associate editor for Carolina Journal, *the monthly newspaper of the John Locke Foundation, an independent think tank.*

A recent report shows that American teenagers regularly engage in a variety of immoral behaviors such as cheating, stealing, and lying. They not only engage in these behaviors, but also do not apparently believe they are immoral compared to others, with the vast majority of teens believing that they act better than most people. A variety of theories regarding the cause of this increase in immorality among young people exist, but the true source of the behavior is public school. Public schools do not teach objective morality; they perpetuate an immoral culture, leading to children who have no moral compass.

Most of us stole something as kids: a pack of gum from the supermarket, a toy car or doll of pocketable size from Wal-Mart, maybe a few quarters from our parents when they weren't looking. My own sortie into criminal life was less glamorous, and definitely less rewarding. At 6 years old, I swiped a plastic PVC pipe from the local hardware store. My dad didn't buy the excuse that I planned to use the pipe to jump-start a career in plumbing, but he did tan my backside for my trouble.

David N. Bass, "Generation Cheat," *The American Spectator*, December 15, 2008. Reproduced by permission.

That taught me the age-old ethic of respect for the private property of others. By my seventh year of life, my stealing ways were ended thanks to parents who tempered my natural depravity with instruction. "Thou shalt not steal," says the Bible in both Old and New Testaments, and the principle has been foundational to civilizations since the dawn of time.

The Morality of Teens

Too bad a growing number of American youth never learned it. According to a new report from the Los Angeles–based Josephson Institute, cheating, stealing, and lying are common pastimes for some youth. One-third of teenagers say they shoplifted in the past year, and about a quarter admit to stealing from parents, relatives, or friends during the same period.

The study, which surveyed the moral beliefs and conduct of almost 30,000 high school students, also found that most teenagers have an inflated view of their own virtue. Seventy-seven percent of respondents said they are "better than most people" when it comes to doing the right thing. That didn't match the self-reported conduct of teens, which included 42 percent who said they sometimes lie to save money and 64 percent who said they cheated on a test at least once in the last year.

"It's a hole in the moral ozone," said Rich Jarc, executive director of the Josephson Institute. "These young people are going to become our future bankers, government officials, and business leaders."

Cheating, stealing, and lying are common pastimes for some youth.

The Moral Atmosphere

Of course, given current headlines, brushing up on lying, cheating, and stealing is probably a worthwhile pursuit for teens intending to join banking, government, or business (say,

car manufacturing). The past few months [fall 2008] have seen an unholy alliance of pseudo-capitalists and socialist politicians, the former grabbing for taxpayer money and the latter eager to dish it out in exchange for unparalleled control of private industries. In that atmosphere, cooking the books or doling out golden parachutes is not only tolerated but encouraged.

And while we're at it, what's wrong with filching a video game from Target when the Illinois governor almost got away with auctioning off [Barack] Obama's vacant Senate seat to the highest bidder?

I asked Jarc to pinpoint what influences kids to readily accept unethical behavior nowadays. "Some of the factors are the media, the need for parents to sometimes work multiple jobs, and a lot of single-parent households," he said. "Then there is all the pressure that kids feel today to get ahead—a lot of exposure, pressure, and bad modeling."

The Role of Public Schools

All true factors, but none get to the crux of the matter. Surveys of this kind typically blame television, Facebook, little to no parental involvement, lack of role models, and other cultural factors. Few, if any, blame the government-controlled education system. With relativism and pragmatism the chief ethical philosophies taught in the public schools, and a social atmosphere steeped in promiscuous sex, violence, and drugs, why expect teens to have a solid moral compass?

Most teens spend half their waking hours under a form of state instruction that considers traditional morality unconstitutional.

The Josephson Institute found that teens in religious high schools were less likely than their public school counterparts to steal (although the numbers were still high). Home-

educated students were not surveyed, but the results would probably have shown far lower rates of unethical behavior and beliefs since many of those students benefit from significant parental involvement, instruction in traditional ethics, and shielding from such unwholesome cultural influences as Britney [Spears] and Paris [Hilton].

Parents can try to be more involved by switching off the TV in the evening or eating dinner as a family, but the influence is negligible. Most teens spend half their waking hours under a form of state instruction that considers traditional morality unconstitutional. When not at school or doing homework, teens are with their peers or engrossed in media, both of which reinforce lackluster morals. Few parents are willing to do anything about it.

That could mean a bleak future. It took one generation, the Baby Boomers, to upend the social fabric of America and pave the way for political, economic, and social disaster. Imagine how Western society will look when a generation with an atrophying moral conscience takes the reins of power.

9

Public Schools Should Be Abolished to Address Society's Vast Moral Divide

David Gelernter

David Gelernter is a professor of computer science at Yale University, contributing editor at the Weekly Standard, *and author of* Americanism: The Fourth Great Western Religion.

America has no reason why it must have public schools, and tax dollars could be spent on supporting private schools from which each parent could choose. Public schools are supposed to be agents of the public, but where there is no consensus on educating children it is impossible for public schools to serve this purpose. A consensus on the role of public schools used to exist— until a couple of decades ago—with the understanding that public schools needed to teach skills and character. Such a consensus no longer exists, and schools now often are the source of moral teachings that not all parents approve. Given this lack of consensus, it makes sense for public schools to be eliminated.

Should America have public schools, or would we do better without them? Nothing is more important to this country than the transformation of children into educated American citizens. That's what public schools are for, and no institutions are better suited to the role—in principle. They used to fill it with distinction.

But there's no reason we *must* have public schools. Granted, the public has a strong interest in educating Amer-

David Gelernter, "A World Without Public Schools," *The Weekly Standard*, vol. 12, no. 36, June 4, 2007, pp. 29–35. Copyright © 2007, News Corporation, Weekly Standard. All rights reserved. Reproduced by permission.

ica's children, at a cost that's divided equitably among all tax-payers and not borne by the parents of school-age children alone. But these requirements don't imply any need for public schools. We need an Air Force, and the Air Force needs planes. Taxpayers pay for the force and the planes. But the pilots are supplied directly by the government, the airplanes by private companies (with government oversight and assistance). Schooling might be furnished on either model: mainly by public or mainly by private organizations. We know that private schools are perfectly capable of supplying first-class educations. So the question stands: Why have public schools? How should we decide whether to have them or not?

Vouchers have been a popular and promising (and controversial) idea for years. Under voucher plans, the public pays part or all of the bill when a child attends private school. But here I am talking about the whole hog, not just the tail and a couple of trotters. If sending *some* children to private school at public expense is worth discussing, why not sending *all* children to private school?

There's no reason we must *have public schools.*

Why not liberate *all* the vast resources we spend on public schools to be rechanneled to private schools chosen by the nation's parents? Any public school offering an education that parents will actually *pay* for (of their own free will) would presumably be replaced by a private school offering essentially the same thing. But a vast array of new private schools would germinate also. And a vast number of failed public schools would disappear.

In the system I am picturing, education would continue to be free and accessible to every child, and all taxpayers would continue to pay for it. Parents would be guaranteed access to "reasonable" schools that cost them nothing beyond what they pay in taxes. It would all be just like today—except that public schools would have vanished.

Would private organizations be capable of providing enough new schools to replace our gigantic public schools establishment? Private enterprise is alleged to be smarter and more resourceful in America than anywhere else in the world. So let's suppose that private schools can indeed meet the needs of nearly all parents. Do we actually need and want our public schools, or do we keep them around out of fear of the teachers' unions—and habit, like a broken child's toy we are too sentimental to throw away?

The Basic Law of Public Schools

Many sources agree that, on the whole, American public schools are rotten. In 2000, a whopping 12 percent of graduating seniors were rated "proficient" in science, and international surveys rank our graduating seniors 19th overall out of 21 nations. In 2002, the *Washington Post* summarized a different survey: "Nearly six in 10 of the nation's high school seniors lack even a basic knowledge of U.S. history." And so on. Our public schools are widely agreed to be in bad shape. But these are only problems of incompetence. Others cut deeper.

The basic law of public schools is this: *Public schools are first and foremost agents of the public.* They exist to transform children into "educated citizens" *as the public understands this term*—in other words, as a public consensus defines it. Of course the United States is a large country; standards have always differed from state to state. So each state has its own public schools, charged with satisfying the consensus definition of "educated citizen" in that state.

In 1898, Nicholas Murray Butler (soon to be president of Columbia University) described universities in terms that make explicit this connection, one that is almost forgotten today. "In order to become great—indeed, in order to exist at all," he wrote, a university [or public school] must represent the national life and minister to it. When the universities of any country cease to be in close touch with the social life and institutions of the people, and fail to yield to the efforts of those who would readjust them, their days of influence are numbered. The same is true of any system of educational organization.

Public schools even more than universities must "represent the national life and minister to it." They must "minister to" the consensus definition of an educated citizen. And what is a "consensus"? "Unanimity or general agreement on matters of opinion," according to Webster's [dictionary], solid agreement by a large majority.

And in states where there *is* no public consensus or general agreement on the meaning of "educated citizen," public schools are in an impossible position. They can't act for the public if the public can't decide how it should act. This is true without regard to whether the schools are working well or badly.

A Lack of Consensus

Today there are few states or none where a public consensus or general agreement exists on what "educated citizen" means. Schools exist not only to teach skills but to mold character. (Although many object to this old-fashioned language, few Americans disagree that schools must teach an approach to life, a worldview, a moral framework.) The culture war that has been under way since the late '60s is precisely a war over approaches to life and worldviews and moral frameworks. Our politics mirror that divide. In the 2004 presidential election, [John] Kerry and [George W.] Bush differed on politics, but stood also for two different worldviews in the larger sense— Kerry the globalizing man-of-the-world with his European experience versus the plainspoken, ranch-living, Bible-quoting

Bush. In simplest terms, Kerry stood for "globalism," Bush for "Americanism." As between these divergent visions, the country split down the middle.

It's pretty clear that no consensus or general agreement on the nature of education is likely to exist in a country that's so divided. Which suggests in turn that, for now, *the age of the American public school is over.* Obviously we shouldn't make such judgments on the basis of short-term disagreements or divisions. But America's culture war has been under way for a generation at least.

Schools exist not only to teach skills but to mold character.

You might argue that the solution is to have two varieties of public school, roughly "moderate Left" and "moderate Right," each with its own curriculum, textbooks, and standards, and its own version of a worldview or moral framework to teach children. Every neighborhood or local region would vote on Left versus Right local schools. In many areas such elections would be extraordinarily hard-fought and bitter—yet the solution might work, except that the school establishment's bias is so consistently Left (and not moderate Left either) that it seems unlikely we could trust it to operate "moderate Right" schools—or even "neutral" schools, if there were such a thing. (The public schools' bias often shows itself in exactly the form of "neutrality," as I'll discuss. If you declare yourself neutral as between America and her enemies, or normal sexuality and homosexuality, your neutrality in itself is bias.)

Of course this whole analysis might be wrong. Maybe I misunderstand the point of public schools. Was there *ever* a consensus in this country on what an educated citizen should be? Maybe we always have been content for the schools to speak for just one section of American society, never the whole.

But this view is wrong. Once upon a time there was indeed an Age of Consensus on public education, and it is worth remembering.

The Age of Consensus

The American public school enjoyed consensus for roughly a century and a half, from its beginnings in the 1820s through the 1970s. Obviously the existence of segregated schools meant that this Age of Consensus agreed only on *some* things. But the evidence suggests that black parents wanted basically the same things for their children as white parents did for theirs. Segregation (after all) was condemned not for neglecting black culture but for failing the test of equality, failing to supply black students with the same quality of education that white students got. Nor did newly arrived Jewish parents from Eastern Europe, for example, want their children studying Yiddish in public school; they wanted them to learn English and grab hold of American culture with both hands.

During these years there was broad agreement on skills teaching *and* character building (or the teaching of worldviews and moral frameworks). The two areas were intertwined. Since the 1970s, consensus in both departments has fallen apart. Both areas are important, but not equally. Disputes about the teaching of skills can be patched up or compromised. Disputes about morality, worldviews, and character building make public schools untenable.

Samuel Johnson (the great essayist and lexicographer) said virtually the same thing in a different way. "Knowledge of external nature," he wrote, "and the sciences which that knowledge requires or includes, are not the great requirement or the frequent business of the human mind." He continues:

> Whether we provide for action or conversation, whether we wish to be useful or pleasing, the first requirement is the religious and moral knowledge of right and wrong; the next is an acquaintance with the history of mankind.... Prudence

and justice are virtues and excellences of all times and of all places; we are perpetually moralists, but we are geometricians only by chance.

Disputes about morality, worldviews, and character building make public schools untenable.

Which is still true in the 21st century. We remain perpetual moralists, and geometricians only by chance. First our children must learn right from wrong, and how to approach life; then they must learn history (assuming they have already learned how to read and write). If the public can't agree on how to teach these things, it has no business maintaining public schools. And nowadays it can't.

The eleventh edition of the *Encyclopædia Britannica* (1910) is a good guide to American attitudes of roughly a century ago, in the age of consensus. "The great mass of the American people," it reported, "are in entire agreement as to the principles which should control public education; and the points in which the policies of the several states are in agreement are greater, both in number and in importance, than those in which they differ. An American educational system exists, therefore, in spirit and in substance, even though not in form." Once, it was possible to argue that all America agreed on the educational basics.

It's fair to object that the *Britannica* spoke for Middle America, and no doubt overstated the actual degree of consensus. But there must have been some sort of consensus; the public was *not* bitterly divided, was *not* split in half as it is today. The *Encyclopædia* continues: "Formal instruction in manners and morals is not often found, but the discipline of the school offers the best possible training in the habits of truthfulness, honesty, obedience, regularity, punctuality and conformity to order." And by the way, "religious teaching is not permitted, although the exercises of the day are often opened with reading from the Bible, the repetition of the Lord's Prayer and the singing of a hymn."

In the Age of Consensus, public schools taught skills *and* built character in ways the public endorsed. In the 19th century, there was general agreement that "no teaching is worthy of the name if it does not have a moral and ethical end" (according to the eminent progressive educator Francis Parker, 1898). And there was broad agreement on *which* moral standards to uphold, and their rootedness in the nation's religious traditions. . . .

Disagreements in Schools Today

There's reason to believe that when it comes to the all-important issue of teaching worldviews and moral frameworks, American public schools are so sharply and consistently biased, they disqualify themselves for the core task of educating citizens. There are so many ways to see the school establishment's bias. . . .

A notorious 2005 dispute in the schools of Lexington, Mass., is highly revealing. The participants behaved and spoke with memorable directness; a student's father went to jail to make a point. It suggests that our disagreements over education go right down to the ground.

American public schools are so sharply and consistently biased, they disqualify themselves for the core task of educating citizens.

David Parker and his wife Tonia had a 5-year-old son in kindergarten. They got wind of the topics on the kindergarten agenda—and asked to be notified and allowed to remove their son from class when same-sex marriage and similar topics were on the day's syllabus. Mr. Parker went to school to insist. He refused to leave until administrators granted his request.

71

They did not grant it. Instead, after two hours of arguing, they called the police and had him arrested. He spent the night in jail.

Few parents have the courage and persistence of the Parkers. But many are deeply angry at the schools for teaching ideas that specifically contradict their child's moral and religious upbringing. The *Boston Globe* quoted Mrs. Parker: "We're not giving unfettered access to the psyche of our son when he enters the school." Orthodox Jews and many Christians believe that homosexuality is a sin. (Which doesn't mean they are "homophobes" or "hate homosexuals," any more than they hate sinners in general. This ridiculous, mean-spirited libel turns religious doctrine upside down. Both religions teach that the sin is hateful, not the sinner. They also teach that male and female are equally essential in the rearing of children. If Jews or Christians who call homosexuality a sin are "homophobes," supporters of same-sex marriage are misogynists or misanthropes, as the case may be. But none of these ad hominem [attacking the person] accusations is helpful.)

For the schools to take it on themselves to contradict and "correct" the religious and moral instruction parents give their children represents (for many Americans) the height of statist arrogance; and exactly what they have come to expect from today's public schools.

Of course you might reply that if the public *is* deeply divided, public schools ought to step forward and offer a compromise. Ought to help lead the nation to common ground; help close the wound and stop the bleeding. Maybe the schism in public thinking means that we need our public schools now more than ever.

But the schools are not acting as if they want to bridge the great divide. Once more the Parker case is illuminating. Lexington School Committee chairman Thomas Griffiths said: "We don't view telling a child that there is a family out there with two mommies as teaching about homosexuality, heterosexuality, or any kind of sexuality. We are teaching about the realities of where different children come from."

A profoundly ideological statement masquerading as sweet reason. The syllogism "if a thing exists 'out there,' the nation's 5-year-olds must be notified at once" will strike many Americans as cracked. But of course others will applaud Griffiths's statement. We are a divided nation. In America today, *there is no consensus for our public schools to embody. . . .*

What could be healthier for America's public schools than to learn that they might not be immortal after all?

The Elimination of Public Schools

What would the nation look like without public schools? Nearly all existing public school buildings would be leased to private schools. All the private schools in any town or district would discuss programs and fees among themselves (which would not count as illegal price-fixing), and with the public too, via local government or town meetings. Any public school whose staff believes in it would be allowed to keep its building and reorganize on a new basis. Some large public schools, especially high schools, would reorganize as confederacies of separate schools sharing one building: a science and math school, humanities school, arts school, sports school. Many students could attend more than one simultaneously. The Internet's most important role might be to help coordinate such complicated arrangements. (Though it's also true that a well-designed Internet school might attract students from all over the country.)

One final question: Is there any chance that abolition will be acted on, or even discussed? Don't hold your breath. Yet it would take just one prominent (even *medium*-prominent) politician or public figure to get America talking. We desperately need this national discussion. And what could be healthier for America's public schools than to learn that they might not be immortal after all?

10

Performance Values: Why They Matter and What Schools Can Do to Foster Their Development

A Position Paper of the Character Education Partnership (CEP). Abridged version.

The Character Education Partnership is a nonprofit, nonpartisan, nonsectarian coalition of organizations and individuals committed to fostering effective character education in America's schools.

Schools currently face many challenges in preparing students for work and for life. Work is central in human life, and the main place where people learn how to work is in school. Educating students to care about the quality of work in later life may be influenced by how much they care about the quality of their work in school. To promote high-quality work in school, a broader view of character must be embraced. Qualities of character in a person consist of both moral character attributes and performance character attributes. Both are necessary to succeed in school and in life, as research shows, supporting the view that character education is a necessary part of school.

As they come of age in a new century, our children face great and growing challenges. On a global scale, they confront an increasingly interdependent economy, exploding tech-

Character Education Partnership, *Performance Values: Why They Matter and What Schools Can Do to Foster Their Development*, April 2008, pp. 2–4, 7. Abridged version. Copyright © Character Education Partnership (CEP), Leading a National Call to Character, 1025 Connecticut Avenue, NW, Suite 1011, Washington, DC 20036. Telephone: 202-296-7743. Fax: 202-296-7779. www.character.org. Reproduced by permission.

nological change, an environment at risk, and a world still plagued by war, disease, and injustice. In a workplace that offers diminishing job security, their ability to interact well with others and adapt to change will matter more than technical expertise. And in their personal lives, young people face the challenge of building healthy relationships and a life of noble purpose in a culture that is often unsupportive of the highest values of the human spirit.

Schools, charged with preparing students to meet these formidable challenges, face a related yet more immediate set of challenges:

- Maintaining a safe and supportive learning environment

- Achieving adequate yearly progress on external academic standards

- Reducing dropouts (30% nationally, as high as 50% in some urban areas)

- Improving students' performance on international tests

- Helping all students achieve and work to their potential, not just attain better grades or higher test scores.

What kind of character will young people need to meet the challenges they face in school and beyond—and how can schools help them develop it while meeting their own set of challenges?

Our work is one of the most basic ways we affect the quality of other people's lives.

The Role of Work in a Life of Character

"The most important human endeavor," Albert Einstein wrote, "is striving for morality." We are defined by our core ethical values—our integrity, our sense of justice and compassion, and the degree to which we respect the dignity and worth of every member of the human family, especially the most vulnerable among us. Research studies conducted in different cultures around the world have substantiated the universality of core ethical values.

We are also known to others by the quality of our work. The quality of the work we do is influenced by many factors, including our skills, the presence or absence of a supportive human environment, and "performance values" such as diligence, preparation for the task at hand, and commitment to the best of which we are capable. The importance of work in people's lives, and even what is regarded as work, may vary among individuals and cultures. Yet in broad terms, our work is one of the most basic ways we affect the quality of other people's lives. When we do our work well—whether teaching a lesson, repairing a car, caring for the sick, or parenting a child—someone typically benefits. When we do our work poorly, someone usually suffers. The essayist Lance Morrow notes the centrality of work to the human community: "All life must be worked at, protected, planted, replanted, fashioned, cooked for, coaxed, diapered, formed, sustained. Work is the way we tend the world."

Where do we learn to care about the quality of our work and to develop the skills to do it well? To a large extent, in school. In his book, *An Ethic of Excellence: Building a Culture of Craftsmanship with Students*, Ron Berger says that during his nearly 30 years as a public school teacher, he also worked part-time as a carpenter. "In carpentry," he writes, "there is no higher compliment than this: 'That person is a craftsman.' That one word connotes someone who has integrity, knowledge, dedication, and pride in work—someone who thinks carefully and does things well." Berger continues:

> I want a classroom full of craftsmen. I want students whose work is strong and accurate and beautiful. In my classroom, I have students who come from homes full of books and

students whose families own almost no books at all. I have students whose lives are generally easy and students with physical disabilities and health or family problems that make life a struggle. I want them all to be craftsmen. Some may take a little longer; some may need to use extra strategies and resources. In the end, they need to be proud of their work, and their work needs to be worthy of pride.

All of us who teach would like our students to be craftsmen—to think carefully about their work, take pride in it, and produce work that is worthy of pride. Teachers, however, say they often struggle to motivate students to care about the quality of their work.

Students who don't develop an orientation toward doing their best work in school may carry that over later in life. As educators, we recognize that some students' paths toward self-discovery, motivation, and accomplishment may emerge outside of the regular classroom in such venues as the fine arts, vocational arts and sciences, and athletics. By work, we mean all these forms of endeavor that engage a person in effortful and meaningful accomplishment.

In all realms of life, good intentions aren't enough; being our best requires work.

Expanding Our View of Character

As character educators, how can we foster students' capacity to work and commitment to doing their work well, in school and throughout life? First, we must expand our view of character to recognize this important dimension of human development. Human maturity includes the capacity to love and the capacity to work. Character strengths such as empathy, fairness, trustworthiness, generosity, and compassion are aspects of our capacity to love. These qualities make up what we could speak of as "moral character"; they enable us to be our best ethical selves in relationships and in our roles as citizens. Character strengths such as effort, initiative, diligence, self-discipline, and perseverance constitute our capacity to work. These qualities make up what we could speak of as "performance character"; they enable us to achieve, given a supportive environment, our highest potential in any performance context (the classroom, the athletic arena, the workplace, etc.). By differentiating moral character and performance character, we do not intend to "reify" them as separate psychological entities: Indeed, some persons may find it more conceptually helpful to think of these as being two "aspects" of our character rather than two distinct "parts" of character.

The moral and performance aspects of character are mutually supportive. The moral aspects, besides enabling us to treat each other with fairness, respect, and care, ensure that we pursue our performance goals in ethical rather than unethical ways. We don't lie, cheat, steal, or exploit other people in order to succeed; rather, our performance efforts contribute positively to the lives of others. The performance aspects of our character, in turn, enable us to act on our moral values and make a positive difference in the world. We take initiative to right a wrong or be of service to others; we persevere to overcome problems and mend relationships; we work selflessly on behalf of others or for a noble cause, often without recognition or reward. In all realms of life, good intentions aren't enough; being our best requires work.

Both moral and performance character are necessary to achieve the goals for which all schools of character strive. Moral character plays a central role in helping schools create safe and caring environments, prevent peer cruelty, decrease discipline problems, reduce cheating, foster social and emotional skills, develop ethical thinking, and produce public-spirited democratic citizens. Performance character plays a central role in helping schools improve all students' academic achievement, promote an ethic of excellence, reduce dropouts, prepare a competent and responsible workforce, and equip young persons with the skills they will need to lead productive, fulfilling lives and contribute to the common good. Both the moral and performance aspects of character are, of course, needed for *all* of the above pursuits; for example, we must work hard (an aspect of performance character) in order to create and sustain a caring school environment, just as we must build caring relationships (an aspect of moral character) in order to be effective at helping students learn and achieve.

Performance Character

Various studies show the contribution of performance character to human development and achievement. Stanford psychologist Walter Mischel and colleagues conducted a study, popularly known as "the marshmallow test," that assessed the ability of 4-year-olds to delay gratification (an important aspect of performance character) and then assessed the "cognitive and self-regulatory competencies" of these same subjects when they were seniors in high school. The 4-year-olds were each given a marshmallow and a choice: If they ate the marshmallow when the experimenter left the room to run an errand, that was the only marshmallow they got; but if they waited 15 minutes for the experimenter to return, they received a second marshmallow. (Psychologists note that whether a child sees delaying gratification as an appropriate response in a particular situation may be influenced by family, neighborhood, and cultural factors.)

Those who, at age four, had been "waiters" on the marshmallow test, compared to those who did not delay gratification, were subsequently better able as adolescents to make and follow through on plans; more likely to persevere in the face of difficulty; more self-reliant and dependable; better able to cope with stress; better able to concentrate on a task; and more academically competent—scoring, on average, more than 100 points higher on a college entrance exam. Mischel concluded that impulse control in the service of a distant goal is a "meta-ability," affecting the development of many important psychological capacities.

In *Character Strengths and Virtues: A Handbook and Classification*, [psychologists] Christopher Peterson and Martin Seligman present theoretical and empirical support for performance character attributes such as creativity, curiosity, love of learning, and persistence. Recent research on expert performance in the arts and sciences, sports, and games reveals that stars are made, not born. Outstanding performance is the product of years of deliberate practice and coaching—training that develops performance character as well as higher levels of the target skill—rather than the result of innate talent. Longitudinal studies such as *Talented Teenagers: The Roots of Success and Failure* find that adolescents who develop their talent to high levels, compared to equally gifted peers who don't fulfill their potential, show higher levels of such performance character qualities as goal setting and wise time management.

Throughout history, and in cultures around the world, education rightly conceived has had two great goals: to help students become smart and to help them become good.

Two Aspects of Character

Research also helps us understand how the moral and performance aspects of character interact. Studies such as [scholars Anne] Colby and [William] Damon's *Some Do Care: Contemporary Lives of Moral Commitment* reveal both strong performance character (e.g., determination, organization, and creativity) and strong moral character (e.g., a sense of justice, integrity, and humility) working synergistically to account for exemplars' achievements in fields as varied as civil rights, education, business, philanthropy, the environment, and religion. Students themselves affirm the complementary roles of performance character and moral character. When researcher Kathryn Wentzel asked middle school students, "How do you know when a teacher cares about you?" they identified two behavior patterns: The teacher *teaches well* (makes class interesting, stays on task, stops to explain something), and the teacher *treats them well* (is respectful, kind, and fair). In other words, "a caring teacher" models both performance character and moral character. . . .

Throughout history, and in cultures around the world, education rightly conceived has had two great goals: to help students become smart and to help them become good. They need character for both. They need moral character in order to behave ethically, strive for social justice, and live and work in community. They need performance character in order to enact their moral principles and succeed in school and in life. Virtue, as the ancient Greeks pointed out, means human excellence. To be a school of character or a community of character is to strive to be our best and do our best in all areas of our lives.

11

High School Ethics Course Affects Knowledge but Not Values

M. Scott Niederjohn, Kim Nygard, and William C. Wood

M. Scott Niederjohn is an assistant professor of economics and business at Lakeland College, Kim Nygard is a financial accountant, and William C. Wood is an economics professor at James Madison University College of Business.

Education often receives the blame for the ethical transgressions of individuals in society. With the goal of seeing if ethics can be taught in high school, a study was undertaken involving ethics curriculum created for high school economics and other social studies classes. Ethics lessons were created and implemented, and students were tested both before and after ethics instruction. Comparing the students who took part in the ethics lessons with those who did not, the ethics students showed a significant increase in knowledge about ethics. They did not show any change in basic ethical attitudes, however, possibly demonstrating that although ethics courses can increase knowledge, they may not change behavior.

When highly visible lapses in ethics occur, education gets some of the blame. Principals in the U.S. subprime mortgage crisis and the Enron [Corporation] scandal had been educated at Harvard and other elite business schools, where professional and moral ideals had arguably been replaced by a focus on profits at the expense of ethics.

M. Scott Niederjohn, Kim Nygard, and William C. Wood, "Teaching Ethics to High School Students: Virtue Meets Economics," *Social Education*, vol. 73, no. 2, March 2009, pp. 76–78. Copyright © National Council for the Social Studies. Reprinted by permission.

The Templeton Project

A long-standing tradition in ethics education, however, holds that by college or graduate school it is "too late" to teach ethics. A natural question arises: Can we teach ethics earlier, possibly at the high school level? This [viewpoint] reports on a curricular effort titled *Teaching the Ethical Foundations of Economics* by the National Council on Economic Education (NCEE) with just that goal. After several years of development and assessment, materials for teaching ethics in social studies classrooms have been prepared and tested. The early results suggest that in fact students can successfully be taught about ethical issues in economics and other social studies classes.

NCEE's ethics project began with a grant from the John Templeton Foundation naming Jonathan B. Wight of the University of Richmond as principal investigator. "Infusing ethical and moral dimensions into economics cannot wait until students attend college," the original 2004 grant proposal stated.

A design and writing team met in 2005, consisting of a philosopher, a business ethicist, two economists, two university-level economic educators and a high school economics educator. The team developed a series of 10 lessons with visuals and activities. Lessons were class-tested in 2006 and revisions followed. The materials debuted at train-the-trainers institutes in 2007 and were published in 2007. An assessment of student learning was completed in 2008.

The early results suggest that in fact students can successfully be taught about ethical issues in economics and other social studies classes.

The Lessons

The lessons resulting from the NCEE project are suitable for social studies classrooms in general, with only one of them

(Lesson 7 on organ transplantation) requiring knowledge of the basic supply and demand model. The other lessons would be suitable for a range of social studies classes including government, psychology, and sociology.

The first lesson in the series is entitled "Does Science Need Ethics?" In this lesson, students examine how preconceptions affect observation and how ethical judgments affect economic analysis. In the second lesson, "What Is the Difference Between Self-Interest and Greed?" students make, accept, and reject ultimatum offers with candy pieces to distinguish healthy self-interest from greed.

The opening lessons are followed by three lessons specifically concerning the operation of markets. In the first of these, "Do Markets Need Ethical Standards?" students play the roles of doctors and patients to see how enlightened self-interest, duty, and virtue improve economic efficiency. Paired lessons then show the usefulness of markets in rewarding virtuous character traits and the moral limitations of markets for solving resource allocation problems.

Two applied lessons then lead students through controversial social topics: "What Should We Do About Sweatshops?" and "Should We Allow a Market for Transplant Organs?" By the eighth lesson in the series, students are learning about efficiency as an ethical concept through role playing involving the critical shortage of a lifesaving serum. In the ninth lesson, students debate the role of business in directly pursuing policies aimed at promoting social justice, the environment, and other causes.

The final lesson, "What Is Economic Justice?" has students play a Veil of Ignorance [a concept introduced by philosopher John Rawls] game to reveal how altering people's self-interest transforms their vision of economic justice and their positions on government policy issues.

Assessment of Learning

The 2008 learning assessment of the lessons employed a pre- and posttest design with a treatment group (those who used *Ethical Foundations*) and a control group (other students who did not participate). In total, 17 teachers from different schools participated.

Teachers were chosen for the project via a random process. Initially, 390 teachers from across the country that had attended an NCEE-sponsored teacher workshop on the *Ethical Foundations* materials were sent an e-mail describing the assessment project; 53 teachers volunteered to participate. Then a random number process was used to identify 17 teachers who completed the project.

Each teacher received further training in the winter of 2008 in the use of the materials and a briefing on the test instruments and processes via e-mail and phone conversations. The teachers returned to their classrooms in the spring of 2008 and administered pretests before using the lessons. The participating teachers also completed and returned questionnaires about their background and their teaching of *Ethical Foundations*. Finally, after completing the lessons with their students, participating teachers mailed back the posttests and related materials.

By the end of the assessment project, there were 875 complete and usable matched-tests received. The final sample included 789 students exposed to the *Ethical Foundations* materials and 86 students in control groups.

The ethics test instrument was developed from assessment questions in the lessons, adapted questions from earlier NCEE assessments, suggestions from the original curriculum authors' conference, and staff work at two centers for economic education. Questions in the test questions covered a range of subjects including, for example, the differences between normative and positive economic statements, the distinction between rational self-interest and greed, frequently cited causes of sweatshop conditions, and the differing opinions of the chairman of Whole Foods [Market] and economist Milton Friedman on the social obligations of businesses. Included at the end of the knowledge test was a set of four questions to gather information on grade level, gender, background in economics and educational plans. . . .

Students who were exposed to the Ethical Foundations *curriculum saw a statistically significant increase in knowledge of ethics and economics.*

Test Results on Knowledge of Ethics and Economics

For the overall test, students who were exposed to the *Ethical Foundations* curriculum saw a statistically significant increase in knowledge of ethics and economics. In contrast, the control group (as expected) showed no statistically significant increase in knowledge. (In fact, this group showed a marginally significant drop in knowledge.)

The 789 students who took the pretest scored an average of 10.24 out of 25 questions correct, or about 41 percent. After exposure to the *Ethical Foundations* curriculum, the students scored an average of 11.68 out of 25 questions correct, or about 47 percent. This amounted to an improvement of just over six percentage points. This increase was well beyond what could be attributed to chance. Statistically, a change in knowledge this large could be expected to occur by chance less than one ten-thousandth of the time.

Collection of data on student and teacher characteristics permitted some further inferences. Participating teachers had been asked to teach as many of the ten lessons as possible; the maximum taught, however, was eight while the minimum taught was four. As expected, the results indicated positive and statistically significant effects among students who had received greater hours of instruction and a greater number of lessons from the *Ethical Foundations* materials. Each additional lesson of instruction was associated with a gain of 0.774 correctly answered questions, holding other variables constant.

There were also, as expected, large and statistically significant differentials for students with higher educational aspirations. There was no statistically significant gender difference; nor were there statistically significant effects of students having taken more economics course work. Interestingly, students in higher grades did worse on the tests, holding other variables constant, perhaps suggesting this curriculum is most effective with students in the earlier high school grades.

Students' basic ethical attitudes were unchanged after exposure to the curriculum.

Test Results on Attitudes

In addition to questions measuring learning, the students answered a survey about attitudes toward ethical issues. One basic result stood out: that students' basic ethical attitudes were unchanged after exposure to the curriculum. This suggests that though we can teach students how to identify and discuss ethical issues as part of the social studies curriculum in general and the economics curriculum in particular, the personal values that drive their attitudes to ethical issues may be more resistant to change. After extensive development, *Teaching the Ethical Foundations of Economics* provides a positive answer to the question: Can we teach high school students about ethical issues? Beyond that, results are mixed. Change in behavior is still another step removed, but behavioral change is clearly an objective when ethical scandals lead to calls for more teaching of ethics.

It is important not to claim too much for a new set of teaching materials. A modest, and empirically supported, conclusion about *Teaching the Ethical Foundations of Economics* is that it does increase ethical awareness. We believe, based on this, that the new curriculum clearly does no harm, and may do some good in promoting ethical behavior.

12

Ethics Needs to Be Taught Early and Should Be Required in College

Kevin Coupe

Kevin Coupe is the founder of MorningNewsBeat.com, an online retail news site.

Despite all the recent ethics scandals in business, many business schools still do not require ethics courses. Ethics needs to be taught in school to try to prevent ethical lapses that destroy businesses and individual lives. An ethics course in college should be mandatory, but successful ethics education depends upon an ethics education that starts much earlier, both in school and at home. If some of the business leaders involved in recent ethics scandals at major companies had taken an ethics course, perhaps things would have turned out differently.

Not long ago, I had the opportunity to moderate a panel at Western Michigan University's annual food-industry conference in Kalamazoo. The panel was made up of both industry executives and students in the school's food-marketing program, and the goal was to explore generational differences. During the session, we started talking about the values they would seek in corporations where they might go to work, and I asked them if they'd ever taken a business-ethics course.

The answer was no. In fact, they'd never taken a course in any kind of ethics.

The Lack of Ethics Courses

To be honest, I was shocked.

After all, we live in an era when executives at Enron [Corporation] and WorldCom have defined on the front pages of the nation's newspapers the essence of greed and mismanagement, and how ethical lapses can have far-ranging implications that destroy not just companies, but the lives of thousands of people.

In chatting with the professors at Western Michigan after the session, I found out that the school does not have a business-ethics course, but does encourage its teachers to bring ethical issues into other classes, whether in management or accounting or whatever. This approach intrigued me, so I started calling around to other schools where I've spent some time over the years.

Ed McLaughlin, a professor of marketing and director of the Food Industry Management Program at Cornell University, Ithaca, N.Y., told me that his university actually is in the middle of a shift in attitude toward the teaching of business ethics. While traditionally the approach has been to embed ethical discussions into other classes, this will change in the fall semester when a business-ethics course is put on the curriculum. "This is something that young business students need to spend more time thinking about," he said, suggesting that "both approaches are important."

We live in an era when executives at Enron [Corporation] and WorldCom have defined on the front pages of the nation's newspapers the essence of greed and mismanagement.

Rich George, a professor of food marketing at St. Joseph's University, said that while St. Joseph's has long believed in spreading ethical discussions across the curriculum, a specific course in business ethics is available at the graduate level. St.

Joseph's actually has the Pedro Arrupe Center for Business Ethics—perhaps a reflection of the school's Jesuit roots.

Finally, I talked with Tom Gillpatrick of Portland State University (PSU) in Oregon, where he is a professor of marketing, as well as executive director of the school's Food Industry Leadership Center (FILC). Gillpatrick told me that PSU has long required its students to take business ethics, that it is critical to help students to figure out where to draw the ethical lines in their careers. "To me, it is not just teaching ethics, not just teaching right and wrong," he said. "They need to be fast on their feet and they have to be prepared, because ethical challenges are things that tend to hit you out of the blue."

I began to feel a little bit better. But I'm still not sure that we're doing our job as leaders if we don't give the whole issue of business ethics the kind of spotlight it deserves.

Ethics Courses in School

Marianne Jennings is a professor of legal and ethical studies at Arizona State University, and she told me that for some reason, most business schools and companies simply do not understand that their people can be great at business and marketing skills, "but if they have ethical lapses . . . it can destroy a business." Most of the ethical case studies that she sees, Jennings said, "are not close calls, not ethical gray areas." But still, "too many people don't know where the lines are."

You can't teach ethics at the college level to someone who doesn't have any. You have to start the process much earlier—in high school, in elementary school and even before. If parents don't start teaching kids about ethical behavior from the very beginning, there is far less of a chance that these kids will grow up with some sort of ethical compass. And we all can name more than a few business executives who have been in the headlines recently whose parents apparently did a lousy job of teaching their kids the difference between right and wrong.

But I think a required ethics course at the college level is an absolute must—if only because it reinforces the importance of ethical behavior, and creates historical and cultural context. One tends to behave more ethically, I think, when one realizes that we don't each exist in a moral vacuum.

I still remember the ethics course I took 30 years ago at Loyola Marymount University. I remember the discussions, I remember my final paper about how the modern American detective novels of Raymond Chandler and Ross Macdonald have as their protagonists characters who essentially serve as moral and ethical arbiters in a rootless and corrupt society. And, I remember the one-sentence theme of the entire semester: that the most important word in any ethical decision is the word "should."

I think a required ethics course at the college level is an absolute must.

Examples of Lapses in Ethics

There are plenty of companies, I think, where if the leadership had ever used that word, or had been exposed to intense discussions of business ethics, things might have gone differently.

Take Ahold, where a multimillion-dollar accounting fraud came close to wrecking the company. When executives there tacitly approved the idea that the numbers should be fudged to keep the stock price high, do you think the notion of right and wrong ever entered their minds?

Or take Albertsons. This may be a less clear-cut ethical case study, but there you have a senior executive who was brought in to reorganize and reinvigorate the company—and in the end, things went so badly that the company had to be broken up and sold for parts—and still he walked away with tens of millions of dollars in compensation. In this case, I wonder if anyone on the board of directors thought about whether it was right or wrong to reward failure?

Or take Wal-Mart. A discussion of Wal-Mart's business ethics probably would be a course unto itself, but let's just consider the case of its disgraced former vice chairman, Tom Coughlin, who pleaded guilty to tax evasion and fraud charges related to financial mismanagement—all because he apparently was getting money under the table from suppliers. If there was one company where one would have thought this couldn't happen, it would have been Wal-Mart—but it did. Think Tom Coughlin ever thought about right and wrong?

Then again, maybe these folks did think about right and wrong. Maybe they just didn't act upon it.

Novelist Robert B. Parker once wrote, "Most people don't have much trouble seeing what's right or wrong. Doing it is sometimes complicated, but knowing the right thing is usually not so hard."

Suggesting, of course, that in order to be ethical people, we need to have both a conscience and a backbone.

13

Ethics Courses for Students May Not Help but Will Not Hurt

Naomi Goldin

Naomi Goldin is a writer and a former student of Cornell University, where she wrote for the Cornell Daily Sun.

The recent business ethics scandals make clear that America's corporate values are lacking. Surveys show that a high percentage of employees at corporations, from the top to the bottom, are engaged in unethical or illegal activity. Some business schools have started requiring business ethics classes as a response to the scandals, but it is not clear that such courses are helping. Nonetheless, requiring ethics courses of all students, and not just those at business school, could possibly help the state of corporate values in America and, at the very least, will not hurt.

Two days ago [October 23, 2006], former Enron [Corporation] CEO [chief executive officer] Jeffrey Skilling was sentenced to 24 years in prison for his involvement in one of the largest corporate scandals of the decade. Skilling was convicted of federal felony charges including conspiracy, insider trading and securities fraud.

A few weeks ago, Yale [University] student Aleksey Vayner made national headlines for his over-the-top 11-page cover letter and video résumé in which the I-Banking [investment banking] applicant made a number of false claims. Vayner credited himself with running a charitable organization, serving as the CEO of an investment firm and writing a book on the Holocaust. Research by bloggers has shown that all of these claims are fabricated.

And, earlier this month, Hewlett-Packard's former chairwoman, Patricia Dunn, was charged with four felony counts for data mining. In her effort to discover the source of continuous company information leaks, Dunn spied on the home-phone records of fellow board members. Dunn found the director; the lawsuit found Dunn.

The State of Corporate Values

So, what do these current events tell us about the state of America's corporate values? Unfortunately, nothing good. It seems as though a trade-off exists between business ethics and business profits—meaning that one comes at the expense of the other. Of course, there are those of us out there who know that this is simply not the case. In fact, there are plenty of socially responsible corporations and business practices that have their fair share of financial success, such as Ben & Jerry's or DuPont. Still, we cannot hide from the reality of increasing corporate malfeasance in recent times.

In his Business and Professional Speaking course, Professor Brian Earle [of Cornell University] recently discussed a survey taken by the Ethics Officers Association which revealed that an alarming 48 percent of employees have engaged in unethical or illegal activity within the past year. The annual cost of these unethical or illegal actions? $400 billion! Perhaps what is even more disconcerting about white-collar crime, however, is that it occurs at every level.

Like Aleksey Vayner (well alright, maybe not quite like Aleksey Vayner), many job applicants fabricate their past experiences and credentials. According to a study released by Avert Inc., a company that performs background checks, 44 percent of job applicants have falsified information about their work experience or education on their résumés. Therefore, it is not surprising that screening and selection services, such as those offered by Avert, are increasingly used by corporations. (Now might be the right time to change that bullet on your resume from "Spearheaded the development of new financial contract database" to "Participated in the development . . ." . . . just a thought.)

It seems as though a trade-off exists between business ethics and business profits.

Business Ethics Courses

But what should be done about the apparent lack of ethical standards in corporate America? In the wake of recent corporate scandals, some business schools have found that the answer rests with education. More and more universities are instituting courses on ethics and social responsibility. For example, FSU's [Florida State University's] College of Business has created a "Business Ethics and Moral Leadership Course" in order to increase students' awareness of the importance of ethical decision making. Bentley College is recognized for its Center for Business Ethics, which is similar to UC [University of California] Berkeley's Center for Responsible Business in its Haas School of Business. Additionally, Northwestern's Kellogg School of [Management], ranked as the 4th best business school in the U.S. by *U.S. News & World Report*, inserted an ethics segment into the basic organizational leadership course that all students are required to take. And Cornell's undergraduate business program currently offers a two-credit course on Business Choices and Consequence. Yes, business programs all around the country are adding required courses on ethics to their curriculums.

One of my best friends attends the Stern School of Business at New York University [NYU]. She recently informed me that NYU also added a required course on business ethics to their undergraduate program, in which she is currently enrolled. The course, Professional Responsibility and Leadership, "is designed to help students consider the purpose and function of business in society and the ways in which a business profession is incorporated into a successful human life." However, rather than being considered a serious component of the business curriculum, the course seems to offer more comic relief than anything else.

Every so often, particularly when I need a good laugh, my Stern friend will call me with a new story from her ethics class. This is my personal favorite: "Well, today we were learning about [Mahatma] Gandhi's teachings—you know, honesty, peace, leading a simple lifestyle—and one of the brainiacs in my class says to the teacher, 'When you get older and amass wealth, it's not about being rich; it's about knowing your grandkids will go to college or that your kids will have Ferraris too.'" Keep in mind that when this student offered his precious token of insight, he was being completely serious.

The Possible Benefit of Ethics Courses

So, why bother teaching ethics if students are already set in their ways? While we may not know the extent to which these courses may benefit the business world in the future, there is no harm in raising awareness. The effort made by [business] schools such as Stern, Haas and Kellogg to educate students on business ethics is admirable. It may be impossible to change the values of students, but it certainly is possible (and important) to make students aware of proper business practices. Providing students with cases of possible leadership situations and ways to handle business in a responsible manner is crucial to developing the honest CEOs of tomorrow.

Perhaps Cornell should jump on the bandwagon and make Business Ethics a required course in the Applied Economics and Management [AEM] curriculum. After all, with a wide course offering ranging from entrepreneurship to econometrics to estate planning, AEM could surely squeeze in a class on ethics.

It may be impossible to change the values of students, but it certainly is possible (and important) to make students aware of proper business practices.

But why should we limit the study of ethics just to business students? What about students studying government, communications or engineering? Or how about our pre-med and pre-law majors, whose future careers will require them to deal effectively with ethical dilemmas?

I am not sure whether it is Cornell's business to impart an understanding of socially responsible practices in society, but I do think that the importance of ethics could be better stressed. While students should be able to distinguish between right and wrong by now, a little refresher never hurt anyone.

Organizations to Contact

The editors have compiled the following list of organizations concerned with the issues debated in this book. The descriptions are derived from materials provided by the organizations. All have publications or information available for interested readers. The list was compiled on the date of publication of the present volume; the information provided here may change. Be aware that many organizations take several weeks or longer to respond to inquiries, so allow as much time as possible.

Center for the Advancement of Ethics and Character (CAEC)
Boston University School of Education
621 Commonwealth Avenue, Boston, MA   02215
(617) 353-3262 • fax: (617) 353-4351
e-mail: CAEC@bu.edu
Web site: www.bu.edu/sed/caec

The Center for the Advancement of Ethics and Character (CAEC) was founded in 1989 at Boston University with the purpose of addressing the broad range of issues related to young people acquiring sound ethical values and forming good character. The CAEC serves as a resource to help administrators, teachers, and parents become better moral educators. The CAEC performs research and publishes a quarterly newsletter, *Character.*

Character Education Institute
California University of Pennsylvania
250 University Avenue, California, PA   15419
(724) 938-5491
e-mail: paul@cup.edu
Web site: www.cup.edu/education/charactered

The Character Education Institute serves as a resource to the California University of Pennsylvania students and provides character development training to regional organizations. The

Character Education Institute provides character education and principle-based consulting services and training in Pennsylvania. The Character Education Institute maintains a resource center, which contains character education curriculum materials, books, journals, newsletters, audiotapes, and videotapes.

Character Education Partnership (CEP)
1025 Connecticut Avenue NW, Suite 1011
Washington, DC   20036
(800) 988-8081 • fax: (202) 296-7779
Web site: www.character.org

The Character Education Partnership (CEP) is a national advocate and leader for the character education movement, composed of a coalition of organizations and individuals committed to fostering effective character education in schools. CEP conducts on-site professional development for schoolteachers and administrators; holds an annual conference, the National Forum on Character Education; and annually recognizes ten schools or districts as National Schools of Character (NSOC). CEP has many resources available on its Web site, including the publication *CEP's Eleven Principles of Effective Character Education.*

Edutopia, the George Lucas Educational Foundation
PO Box 3494, San Rafael, CA   94912
(415) 662-1673 • fax: (415) 662-1619
e-mail: info@edutopia.org
Web site: www.edutopia.org

Edutopia, the George Lucas Educational Foundation, was created to change education by helping children become lifelong learners and develop the technical, cultural, and interpersonal skills to succeed in the twenty-first century. Edutopia works to spread the word about ideal, interactive learning environments and enable others to adapt these successes locally. Edutopia publishes *Edutopia* magazine and education-related videos, which are available on its Web site.

Ethics Resource Center (ERC)

2345 Crystal Drive, Suite 201, Arlington, VA   22202
(703) 647-2185 • fax: (703) 647-2180
e-mail: ethics@ethics.org
Web site: www.ethics.org

The Ethics Resource Center (ERC) is a private, nonprofit organization devoted to independent research and the advancement of high ethical standards and practices in public and private institutions. ERC researchers analyze current and emerging issues and produce new ideas and benchmarks on ethics and ethical behavior. The ERC publishes research and a newsletter, *Ethics Today*, both of which are available on its Web site.

Heartwood Institute

1133 South Braddock Avenue, Suite C, Pittsburgh, PA   15218
(800) 432-7810 • fax: (412) 723-2661
e-mail: hrtwood@heartwoodethics.org
Web site: www.heartwoodethics.org

Heartwood Institute is a nonprofit educational organization founded to promote the understanding and practice of seven universal ethical attributes: courage, loyalty, justice, respect, hope, honesty, and love. Heartwood Institute provides tools for high-quality, multicultural ethics education and promotes the need for ethics instruction. Heartwood Institute has tools available on its Web site for teaching ethics to children, along with access to its newsletter, *From the Heart.*

Josephson Institute

9841 Airport Boulevard, #300, Los Angeles, CA   90045
(800) 711-2670 • fax: (310) 846-4858
Web site: www.josephsoninstitute.org

The Josephson Institute is a nonpartisan, nonsectarian, nonprofit organization working to improve the ethical quality of society by changing personal and organizational decision making and behavior. The Josephson Institute develops and delivers services and materials to increase ethical commitment, competence, and practice in all segments of society, including its CHARACTER COUNTS! program for character education. The CHARACTER COUNTS! program publishes several free e-newsletters, including *Commentary*, *Pursuing Victory with Honor*, and *CHARACTER COUNTS! Chronicle*.

Peaceful Solution Character Education Incorporated (PSCEI)

PO Box 2442, Abilene, TX   79604
(888) 613-9494 • fax: (325) 677-9023
e-mail: info@peacefulsolution.org
Web site: www.peacefulsolution.org

The Peaceful Solution Character Education Incorporated (PSCEI) is a nonprofit organization devoted to promoting character education as its main tool for positive character development. The PSCEI has developed *The Peaceful Solution® Character Education Program* (PSCEP) with a variety of courses designed to reach all ages, so the impact of character change can be realized and effective in society. PSCEI's Web site offers access to numerous publications and features its Children's Corner, which has online activities aimed at character education.

Bibliography

Books

Gunilla Dahlberg and Peter Moss — *Ethics and Politics in Early Childhood Education*. New York: RoutledgeFalmer, 2005.

Sara Dimerman — *Character Is the Key: How to Unlock the Best in Our Children and Ourselves*. Hoboken, NJ: Wiley, 2009.

Julie Duckworth — *The Little Book of Values: Educating Children to Become Thinking, Responsible and Caring Citizens*. Ed. Ian Gilbert. Bethel, CT: Crown House Publishing, 2009.

Miriam Grossman — *You're Teaching My Child What? A Physician Exposes the Lies of Sex Education and How They Harm Your Child*. Washington, DC: Regnery Publishing, 2009.

Thomas C. Hunt and Monalisa Mullins — *Moral Education in America's Schools: The Continuing Challenge*. Greenwich, CT: Information Age Publishing, 2005.

William H. Jeynes — *A Call for Character Education and Prayer in the Schools*. Santa Barbara, CA: Praeger, 2009.

Liz Knowles and Martha Smith — *Character Builders: Books and Activities for Character Education.* Westport, CT: Libraries Unlimited, 2006.

Daniel K. Lapsley and F. Clark Power, eds. — *Character Psychology and Character Education.* Notre Dame, IN: University of Notre Dame Press, 2005.

Stephen Law — *The War for Children's Minds.* New York: Routledge, 2006.

Judd Kruger Levingston — *Sowing the Seeds of Character: The Moral Education of Adolescents in Public and Private Schools.* Westport, CT: Praeger, 2009.

Larry P. Nucci and Darcia Narvaez, eds. — *Handbook of Moral and Character Education.* New York: Routledge, 2008.

Josephine Russell — *How Children Become Moral Selves: Building Character and Promoting Citizenship in Education.* Portland, OR: Sussex Academic Press, 2007.

H. Svi Shapiro — *Losing Heart: The Moral and Spiritual Miseducation of America's Children.* Mahwah, NJ: Lawrence Erlbaum Associates, 2006.

H. Svi Shapiro, ed. — *Education and Hope in Troubled Times: Visions of Change for Our Children's World.* New York: Routledge, 2009.

| Peter Smagorinsky and Joel Taxel | *The Discourse of Character Education: Culture Wars in the Classroom.* Mahwah, NJ: Lawrence Erlbaum Associates, 2005. |

Periodicals

| Carol Gerber Allred | "Improving Academics: Behavior and Character," *Leadership*, November–December 2008. |

| Sara Bernard | "Moral Aptitude," *Edutopia*, August 2008. |

| Hunter Brimi | "Academic Instructors or Moral Guides? Moral Education in America and the Teacher's Dilemma," *Clearing House: A Journal of Educational Strategies, Issues and Ideas*, January–February 2009. |

| Colleen Carroll Campbell | "God and the Public Schools," *Lay Witness Magazine*, September–October 2006. |

| Mona Charen | "Character Counts, but Not by Race," *National Review Online*, April 11, 2008. www.nationalreview.com. |

| *Current Events* | "Curses! Should Students Be Fined for Using Foul Language?" January 20, 2006. |

| Derek H. Davis | "Character Education in America's Public Schools," *Journal of Church and State*, Winter 2006. |

Selwyn Duke   "Schooling in the Third Millennium:
                     Bible Out, Sodom In," *New American*,
                     June 10, 2009.
                     www.thenewamerican.com.

Greg Farrell   "Bad Harvard Grads Are Poster Boys
                     for Ethics Classes," *USA Today*,
                     September 28, 2006.

Stanley Fish   "Professor, Do Your Job," *Policy
                     Review*, August–September 2008.

Marc Fisher   "A Report on Moral Character Best
                     Left Behind," *Washington Post*, April
                     10, 2008.

Amy Haas   "Now Is the Time for Ethics in
                     Education," *CPA Journal*, June 2005.

Charles C. Haynes "Schools of Conscience," *Educational
                     Leadership*, May 2009.

Frederick M. Hess "Do Student Rights Interfere with
                     Teaching and Learning in Public
                     Schools?" *CQ Researcher*, June 1,
                     2009.

Rushworth M.   "Lying in the Big Leagues," *Education
Kidder   Canada*, Summer 2009.

Paul Kurtz   "Wanted: Moral Education for
                     Secular Children," *Free Inquiry*,
                     December–January 2007.

Tibor R. Machan   "Schools Without the State?" *Free
                     Inquiry*, August–September 2007.

Edward Monsour   "Teaching Ethics to Accounting
                     Majors," *Tax Adviser*, May 2007.

Melissa L. Morgan — "Character Matters for Kids," *Practical Homeschooling*, January–February 2008.

Bill O'Reilly — "Don't Kid Around in the Classroom," *Jewish World Review*, May 16, 2005.

Susan Pass and Wendy Willingham — "Teaching Ethics to High School Students," *Social Studies*, January–February 2009.

Andre M. Perry — "Why Schools Must Teach Morality," *Times-Picayune* (New Orleans, LA), January 31, 2009.

Cheryl Poole — "Students Would Benefit from Moral Guidance," *Augusta Chronicle* (Augusta, GA), November 9, 2008.

Grace Rubenstein — "How to Teach Character in the Classroom," *Edutopia*, June 2006.

Andrea Batista Schlesinger — "Three R's and a Why," *Nation*, September 15, 2009. www.thenation.com.

Kevin Sullivan — "Character Education: Models of Imperfection," *School Arts*, April 2007.

Lynn Vincent — "Bible Basics: Two Programs to Teach Scripture in Public Schools Move Ahead," *World*, November 4, 2006.

Will Wilkinson — "The Real School Indoctrination Scandal," *The Week*, September 16, 2009.

Index